Thoreau: A Century of Criticism

Thoreau

A CENTURY OF CRITICISM

EDITED BY

WALTER HARDING
Secretary of the Thoreau Society

SOUTHERN METHODIST UNIVERSITY PRESS: DALLAS

To
David, Allen, Larry, and Susan

PREFACE

I have attempted to compress into this volume the major pieces of criticism of the writings of Henry David Thoreau that have appeared in the century since George Ripley wrote the earliest review of Thoreau's first book for the *New York Tribune* of June 13, 1849. Needless to say, it has proved impossible to include everything that has been written about Thoreau; but I have tried to present the most influential pieces, including at least one study of each of his major works, one study in each of his major fields of interest, at least one essay from each decade of the past hundred years representative of the gradual change in critical opinion of the man, and a proportionate balance between negative and positive criticism.

Because the material available for such a volume is so large, I have set up the following standards for selection: I have eliminated all those essays which are primarily biographical rather than critical, those which are essentially source studies, and excerpts from any of the book length studies of Thoreau. It is inevitable that I have been unable to include many works which one might like to see represented in this volume. But it is my hope that these omissions have been made necessary by the limitations of the volume and not by my oversight. It is also my hope that the student will find here an adequate representation of critical opinion of Thoreau and the beginner a good introduction to his writings.

The essays are arranged in chronological order. Each is reproduced as first printed with the exceptions that obvious typographical errors have been corrected and a few long quotations from Thoreau's works and several lengthy digressions have been deleted. These deletions in no way, I feel, change the tenor of the remarks, and each such deletion has been indicated by the usual ellipsis.

A brief introduction attempts to point out the general pattern of Thoreau criticism. A few background comments introduce each essay.

This opportunity is taken to return special thanks to those who have so generously granted permission to reprint copyrighted essays—Miss Marianne Moore of the Dial Publishing Company, for the lines from Gilbert P. Coleman's "Thoreau and His Critics" quoted in my introduction; to Mrs. Harry Fine and the *Atlantic Monthly* for Paul Elmer More's "A Hermit's Notes on Thoreau"; to the *Atlantic Monthly* and Charlotte W. Hardy, for Fannie Hardy Eckstorm's "Thoreau's 'Maine Woods' "; to Waldo Frank, for "Henry David Thoreau (1817-1917)"; to the *Sewanee Review* and Norman Foerster, for "Thoreau as Artist"; to H. M. Tomlinson, for "Thoreau" from "Two Americans and a Whale"; to Alyse Gregory, for Llewelyn Powys' "Thoreau: A Disparagement"; to the *New Statesman and Nation* and Catherine Salt, for Henry S. Salt's "Gandhi and Thoreau"; to *Newsweek* and Random House, for Sinclair Lewis' "One Man Revolution"; to *American Literature* and Henry W. Wells, for "An Evaluation of Thoreau's Poetry"; to James Ladd Delkin and Henry Miller, for "Preface to *Three Essays by Henry David Thoreau";* to the *Atlantic Monthly* and Stanley Edgar Hyman, for "Henry Thoreau in Our Time"; to the *New York Herald Tribune* and Alfred Kazin, for "Thoreau's Journals"; and to the *Scientific Monthly* and Mr. and Mrs. Philip B. Whitford for "Thoreau: Pioneer Ecologist and Conservationist."

WALTER HARDING

Charlottesville, Virginia
August 9, 1954

CONTENTS

CONTENTS

Thoreau: A Century of Criticism

INTRODUCTION

As is the case with criticism of any genuinely original figure in literature, the criticism of Thoreau is characterized by little agreement or uniformity. He has been damned as loudly as he has been praised—and praised as loudly as damned. Worse yet, even those who admire him most cannot agree on either his strong or his weak points. As a critic of Thoreau's critics has said:

> It is amusing, and occasionally startling, to observe the infinite variety of criticism that has been stirred up by Thoreau's life and works. Many writers, for example, are agreed in describing his temperament as ascetic. Robert Louis Stevenson, however, is not alone in holding the opposite view. "He was not ascetic," says Stevenson, "rather an Epicurean of the nobler sort." Professor Nichols, in his little work on American Literature, apparently is satisfied with middle ground, when he applies to Thoreau the classification, "lethargic, self-complacently defiant, too nearly a stoico-epicurean adiaphorist to discompose himself in party or even in national strifes." Nearly all the critics are agreed that Thoreau was a humorist, though they are by no means agreed as to the quality of his humor. Another school, headed by Lowell, is quite certain that he possessed no humor whatever. One writer speaks of him as "repellent, cold, and unamiable," while another declares that "in all social relations he was guided by a fine instinct of courtesy," and Emerson, who knew him nearly as well as anybody ever did, says that "he was really fond of sympathy"; a highly appreciative essayist speaks of the "fine resonant quality of his emotional side," and finds that he was "always thoroughly kindly and sympathetic."

These comments were written nearly half a century ago, but still the controversy rages.

Yet there is more pattern to the criticism than these comments might indicate. Thoreau's writings were pretty much ignored in his

1

lifetime. *A Week* received only two notices of any length. *Walden* received but few more. With certain exceptions, most of these reviews were unfriendly. Thoreau could not have been greatly cheered by most of the criticism he read.

When Emerson published his funeral sermon for Thoreau, extolling him as a New England Stoic, he quite unintentionally set up an unfavorable pattern. For years after that his friend was dismissed as cold, humorless, a skulker, one "who picked strawberries in Emerson's own garden." But slowly the tide turned in his favor. First it was the nature lovers who discovered him. They dismissed his philosophy as worthless, but delighted in his description of the great outdoors. They extolled his "wildness" and quoted lovingly from his battle of the ants. The publication of four volumes of comments on the seasons excerpted from his journals in the 1880's and 1890's added to this interest.

Gradually, however, more penetrating critics began to see in him more than a mere nature writer. As was the case with Melville, the English critics set the pace for Thoreau's own countrymen. Perhaps the publication of Henry S. Salt's biography in 1890 did more than anything else to point the way. With the publication of the complete journals in 1906, the general reader was able to discover for himself that Thoreau was more fundamentally a philosopher than a naturalist. But perhaps most of all it was the depression of the 1930's that really established him in the front rank of American authors. He was one of the rare authors that a poor man could read without being insulted. At any rate, he has arrived. He has been claimed by groups as diverse as anarchists and limnologists. There are still those who dissent. He has yet to be elected to the Hall of Fame or honored by his alma mater, Harvard. But his place is unquestionably secure among the few great American authors.

[1849]

When Thoreau's first book, A Week on the Concord and Merrimack Rivers, *was published, the first review of the book to reach
print appeared in Horace Greeley's* New York Tribune. *Greeley
had known Thoreau for some years and acted as his literary agent
in placing magazine articles. George Ripley, the reviewer, a former
Unitarian minister and the founder of Brook Farm, had long
known Thoreau personally and here took him to task for his
pantheism. It was this unorthodoxy in religion which probably so
limited sales of the book.*

A WEEK ON THE CONCORD AND MERRIMACK RIVERS

A Review

BY GEORGE RIPLEY

A really new book—a fresh, original, thoughtful work—is sadly
rare in this age of omniferous publication. Mr. Thoreau's, if not
entirely this, is very near it. Its observations of Nature are as genial
as Nature herself, and the tones of his harp have an Aeolian
sweetness. His reflections are always striking, often profoundly
truthful, and his scholastic treasures, though a little too ostenta-
tiously displayed, are such as the best instructed reader will enjoy
and thank him for. His philosophy, which is the Pantheistic egotism
vaguely characterized as Transcendental, does *not* delight us. It
seems secondhand, imitative, often exaggerated—a bad specimen

---

From the *New York Tribune,* June 13, 1849. Several long quotations from the book
and one from the *Edinburgh Review* presenting George Ripley's views on the Bible
have been omitted.

3

of a dubious and dangerous school. But we will speak first of the staple of the work.

Mr. Thoreau is a native and resident of Concord, Massachusetts —a scholar, a laborer, and in some sort a hermit. He traveled somewhat in his earlier years (he is still young), generally trusting to his own thoughts for company and his walking-cane for motive power. It would seem a main purpose of his life to demonstrate how slender an impediment is poverty to a man who pampers no superfluous wants, and how truly independent and self-sufficing is he who is in no manner the slave of his own appetites. Of his fitful hermit life and its results we have already given some account: Now for his "Week on the Concord and Merrimac."

The Concord is a dull, dark, sluggish creek or petty river which runs through the Massachusetts town of that name and is lost in the Merrimac at Lowell. On this stream, Mr. Thoreau and his friend embarked one Autumn afternoon in a small rowboat, and rowed or sailed down to the dam near its mouth, thence across by the old Middlesex Canal to the Merrimac above Lowell, thence up the latter to Hooksett, New Hampshire, where they left their boat and varied their experience by a pedestrian tour through the wild and rugged heart of the Granite State, returning to their boat after a week's absence and retracing their course homeward. They had a tent which, while boating, they pitched in the most inviting and secluded spot—generally a wood, when night overtook them— they cooked and served for themselves, only approaching the dwellings rarely to purchase milk or fruit or bread. Such is the thread of the narrative: let us give a single specimen of its observations of Nature. . .

Whether we live by the sea-side, or by the lakes and rivers or on the prairie, it concerns us to attend to the nature of fishes, since they are not phenomena confined to certain localities only, but forms and phases of the life in nature universally dispersed. The countless shoals which annually coast the shores of Europe and America, are not so interesting to the student of nature as the more fertile law itself, which deposits their spawn on the tops of mountains, and on the interior plains; the fish principle in nature, from which it results that they may be found in water in so many places, in greater or less numbers. The natural historian is not a fisherman, who prays for cloudy days and good luck merely, but as fishing has been styled, "A contemplative man's recreation," introducing him profitably to woods and water, so the fruit of the naturalist's observations is not in new genera or species, but in new contemplations still, and science is only a more contemplative man's recreation. The seeds of the life of fishes are everywhere disseminated, whether the winds waft them, or the waters float them, or the deep earth holds them; wherever a pond is dug, straightway it is stocked with this vivacious race. They have a lease of nature, and it is not yet out. The Chinese are bribed to carry their ova from province to province in jars or in hollow reeds, or the water-birds to transport them to the mountain tarns and interior lakes. There are fishes wherever there is a fluid medium, and even in clouds and in melted metals we detect their semblance. Think how in Winter you can sink a line down straight in a pasture through snow and through ice, and pull up a bright, slippery, dumb, subterranean silver or golden fish! It is curious, also, to reflect how they make one family from the largest to the smallest. The least minnow, that lies on the ice as bait for pickerel, looks like a huge sea-fish cast up on the shore. . . .

Half the book is like and as good as this.—Nearly every page is instinct with genuine Poetry except those wherein verse is haltingly attempted, which are for the most part sorry prose. Then there is a misplaced Pantheistic attack on the Christian Faith. Mr. Thoreau—we must presume soberly—says:

In my Pantheon, Pan still reigns in his pristine glory, with his ruddy face, his flowing beard, and his shaggy body, his pipe and his crook, his nymph Echo, and his chosen daughter Iambe; for the great god Pan is not dead, as was rumored. Perhaps of all the gods of New England and of ancient Greece, I am most constant at his shrine.

One memorable addition to the old mythology is due to this era,—the Christian fable. With what pains, and tears, and blood, these centuries have woven this and added it to the mythology of mankind. The new Prometheus. With what miraculous consent, and patience, and persistency, has this mythus been stamped upon the memory of the race? It would seem as if it were in the progress of our mythology to dethrone Jehovah, and crown Christ in his stead.

If it is not a tragical life we live, then I know not what to call it. Such a story as that of Jesus Christ,—the history of Jerusalem, say, being a part of the Universal History. The naked, the embalmed, unburied death of Jerusalem amid its desolate hills,—think of it. In Tasso's poem I trust some things are sweetly buried. Consider the snappish tenacity with which they preach Christianity still. What are time and space to Christianity, eighteen hundred years, and a new world?—that the humble life of a Jewish peasant should have force to make a New-York bishop so bigoted. Forty-four lamps, the gift of kings, now burning in a place called the Holy Sepulchre;—a church bell ringing; —some unaffected tears shed by a pilgrim on Mount Calvary within the week.

"Jerusalem, Jerusalem, when I forget thee, may my right hand forget her cunning."

"By the waters of Babylon there we sat down, and we wept when we remembered Zion."

I trust that some may be as near and dear to Buddha, or Christ, or Swedenborg, who are without the pale of their churches. It is necessary not to be Christian, to appreciate the beauty and significance of the life of Christ. I know that some will have hard thoughts of me, when they hear their Christ named beside my Buddha, yet I am sure that I am willing they should love their Christ more than my Buddha, for the love is the main thing, and I like him too. Why need Christians be still intolerant and superstitious?

The reading which I love best is the Scriptures of the several nations, though it happens that I am better acquainted with those of the Hindoos, the Chinese, and the Persians, than of the Hebrews, which I have come to last. Give me one of these Bibles, and you have silenced me for a while.

We have quoted a fair proportion of our author's smartest Pantheistic sentences, but there is another in which he directly asserts that he considers the Sacred Books of the Brahmins in nothing inferior to the Christian Bible. It was hardly necessary to say in addition that he is not well acquainted with the latter—the point worth considering is rather—*ought not* an author to *make himself* thoroughly acquainted with a book, which, if true, is of such transcendent importance, before uttering opinions concerning it calculated to shock and pain many readers, not to speak of those who will be utterly repelled by them? Can that which Milton and Newton so profoundly reverenced (and they *had* studied it thoroughly) be wisely turned off by a youth as unworthy of even consideration? Mr. Thoreau's treatment of this subject seems revolting alike to good sense and good taste. . . .

Albeit we love not theologic controversy, we proffer our columns to Mr. Thoreau, should he see fit to answer these questions. We would have preferred to pass the theme in silence, but our admiration of his book and our reprehension of its Pantheism forbade that course. May we not hope that he will reconsider his too rashly expressed notions on this head?

[1854]

Unquestionably the best criticism of Thoreau's writings that appeared in his lifetime has lain forgotten in the files of an obscure antislavery newspaper. Although Thoreau mentioned it favorably in a letter to his devoted disciple H. G. O. Blake, it has escaped the attention of bibliographers and students alike. Unfortunately it is unsigned, and there seems to be no way of identifying its author.

THOREAU'S WALDEN

ANONYMOUS

These books spring from a depth of thought which will not suffer them to be put by, and are written in a spirit in striking contrast with that which is uppermost in our time and country. Out of the heart of practical, hard-working, progressive New England come these Oriental utterances. The life exhibited in them teaches us, much more impressively than any number of sermons could, that this Western activity of which we are so proud, these material improvements, this commercial enterprise, this rapid accumulation of wealth, even our external, associated philanthropic action, are very easily overrated. The true glory of the human soul is not to be reached by the most rapid travelling in car or steamboat, by the instant transmission of intelligence however far, by the most speedy accumulation of a fortune, and however efficient measures we may adopt for the reform of the intemperate, the emancipation of the enslaved, &c., it will avail little unless we are ourselves essentially noble enough to inspire those whom we would so benefit with

From the *National Anti-Slavery Standard*, December 16, 1854, p. 3.

nobleness. External bondage is trifling compared with the bondage of an ignoble soul. Such things are often said, doubtless, in pulpits and elsewhere, but the men who say them are too apt to live just with the crowd, and so their words come more and more to ring with a hollow sound.

It is refreshing to find in these books the sentiments of one man whose aim manifestly is to *live,* and not to waste his time upon the externals of living. Educated at Cambridge, in the way called liberal, he seems determined to make a liberal life of it, and not to become the slave of any calling, for the sake of earning a reputable livelihood or of being regarded as a useful member of society. He evidently considers it his first business to become more and more a living, advancing soul, knowing that thus alone (though he desires to think as little as possible about that) can he be, in any proper sense, useful to others. Mr. Thoreau's view of life has been called selfish. His own words, under the head of "Philanthropy" in Walden, are the amplest defense against this charge, to those who can appreciate them. In a deeper sense than we commonly think, charity begins at home. The man who, with any fidelity, obeys his own genius, serves men infinitely more by so doing, becoming an encouragement, a strengthener, a fountain of inspiration to them, than if he were to turn aside from his path and exhaust his energies in striving to meet their superficial needs. As a thing by the way, aside from our proper work, we may seek to remove external obstacles from the path of our neighbours, but no man can help them much who makes that his main business, instead of seeking evermore, with all his energies, to reach the loftiest point which his imagination sets before him, thus adding to the stock of true nobleness in the world.

But suppose all men should pursue Mr. Thoreau's course, it is asked triumphantly, as though, then, we should be sure to go back to barbarism. Let it be considered, in the first place, that no man could pursue his course who was a mere superficial imitator, any more than it would be a real imitation of Christ if all men were to make it their main business to go about preaching the Gospel to each other. Is it progress toward barbarism to simplify one's outward life for the sake of coming closer to Nature and to the realm of ideas? Is it civilization and refinement to be occupied evermore with adding to our material conveniences, comforts and luxuries, to make ourselves not so much living members as dead tools of society, in some bank, shop, office, pulpit or kitchen? If men were to follow in Mr. Thoreau's steps, by being more obedient to their loftiest instincts, there would, indeed, be a falling off in the splendor of our houses, in the richness of our furniture and dress, in the luxury of our tables, but how poor are these things in comparison with the new grandeur and beauty which would appear in the souls of men. What fresh and inspiring conversation should we have, instead of the wearisome gossip, which now meets us at every turn. Men toil on, wearing out body or soul, or both, that they may accumulate a needless amount of the externals of living; that they may win the regard of those no wiser than themselves; their natures become warped and hardened to their pursuits; they get fainter and fainter glimpses of the glory of the world, and, by and by, comes into their richly-adorned parlours some wise and beautiful soul, like the writer of these books, who, speaking from the fullness of his inward life, makes their luxuries appear vulgar, showing that, in a direct way, he has obtained the essence of that which his entertainers have been vainly seeking for at such a terrible expense.

It seems remarkable that these books have received no more adequate notice in our Literary Journals. But the class of scholars are often as blind as others to any new elevation of soul. In Putnam's Magazine, Mr. Thoreau is spoken of as an oddity, as the Yankee Diogenes, as though the really ridiculous oddity were not in us of the "starched shirt-collar" rather than in this devotee of Nature and Thought. Some have praised the originality and profound sympathy with which he views natural objects. We might as well stop with praising Jesus for the happy use he has made of the lilies of the field. The fact of surpassing interest for us is the simple grandeur of Mr. Thoreau's position—a position open to us all, and of which this sympathy with Nature is but a single result. This is seen in the less descriptive, more purely thoughtful passages, such as that upon Friendship in the "Wednesday" of the "Week," and in those upon "Solitude," "What I Lived for," and "Higher Laws," in "Walden," as well as in many others in both books. We do not believe that, in the whole course of literature, ancient and modern, so noble a discourse upon Friendship can be produced as that which Mr. Thoreau has given us. It points to a relation, to be sure, which, from the ordinary level of our lives, may seem remote and dreamy. But it is our thirst for, and glimpses of, such things which indicate the greatness of our nature, which give the purest charm and colouring to our lives. The striking peculiarity of Mr. Thoreau's attitude is, that while he is no religionist, and while he is eminently practical in regard to the material economics of life, he yet manifestly feels, through and through, that the loftiest dreams of the imagination are the solidest realities, and so the only foundation for us to build upon, while the affairs in which men are everywhere busying themselves so intensely are comparatively the merest froth and foam.

[1857]

When the anonymous English critic sat down to write this first
lengthy notice of Thoreau across the Atlantic, he cribbed whole
sections of it from two American reviews: "A Yankee Diogenes"
by Charles Frederick Briggs in the October, 1854, Putnam's
Monthly *and "Town and Rural Humbugs," an anonymous notice*
in the March, 1855, Knickerbocker Magazine. *It thus gives a*
good cross section of the reception of Walden.*

AN AMERICAN DIOGENES

ANONYMOUS

When Philip of Macedon announced his intention to invade
Corinth, the inhabitants of that city, overlooking, or feigning not
to perceive, their utter incapability of resistance, affected to make
great preparations for defence; while Diogenes, who, like many of
us, even at the present time, delighted to ridicule the follies he did
not himself commit, rolled about his tub in an excited, bustling
manner, by way of deriding the fussy, fruitless show of opposition
made by the feeble Corinthians. The transatlantic Diogenes, however, when he observed the foolish, aimless bustle made by the
modern Corinthians of the world, in pursuit of the sacred dollar
and its glittering accessories, instead of rolling about his tub,
quietly sat down in it, and wrote an interesting book, replete with
pithy, original observations, but strongly tinctured with the inevitable dogmatism that ever attends the one *soi-disant* wise man who
assumes to be the teacher of all the rest of his race. Henry D.
Thoreau, the American Diogenes, if we may presume to term him

From *Chambers's Journal,* VIII (November 21, 1857), 330-32.

12

so—assuredly we mean no offence—is a graduate of Harvard university, a ripe scholar, and a transcendentalist of the Emersonian school, though he goes much further than his master; his object, apparently, being the exaltation of mankind by the utter extinction of civilisation. When Nat Lee was confined in Bedlam, the unfortunate dramatist roundly asserted his perfect sanity, exclaiming: 'All the world say that I am mad, but I say that all the world are mad; so being in the minority, I am placed here.' Now, the truth, as it generally does, may have lain between the two extremes; and in like manner, Mr. Thoreau, when he lazily lived in a hut, in a lonely wood, subsisting on beans, was not half so mad as his neighbours, the 'cute New Englanders, supposed to him to be; nor, on the other hand, were they so mad as he considered them, though they lived in comfortable houses, in towns, and ate beef and mutton, which they consequently worked hard to pay for.

Mr. Thoreau had 'tried school-keeping,' but without success, because he 'did not teach for the good of his fellow-men, but simply for a livelihood.' He had tried commerce, but found 'that trade curses everything it handles; and though you trade in messages from heaven, the whole curse of trade attaches to the business.' He had tried 'doing good,' but felt satisfied that it did not agree with his constitution. Indeed he says: 'The greater part of what my neighbors call good, I believe in my soul to be bad; and if I repent of anything, it is very likely to be my good-behavior.' At last, as he could fare hard, and did not wish to spend his time in earning rich carpets or other fine furniture, or a house in the Grecian or Gothic style, he concluded that 'the occupation of a day-labourer was the most independent of any, especially as it required only thirty or forty days' work to support a man for the whole year. Besides, the labourer's day ends with the going down of the sun, and he is then free to devote himself to his chosen pursuit; but his employer, who speculates from month to month, has no respite from one end of the year to the other.' So, borrowing an axe, he boldly marched into the woods of Concord, where, on the pleasant bank of Walden Pond, he built himself a hut, in which he lived alone for more than two years, subsisting chiefly on beans planted and gathered by his own hands. In the book, already adverted to, his thoughts and actions during this period are pleasantly and interestingly related; though, like all solitary men, the author exaggerates the importance of his own thoughts, his *I* standing up like an obelisk in the midst of a level, though by no means barren expanse.

The building of his hut gave rise to many reflections. He wondered that in all his walks he never came across a man engaged in so simple and natural an occupation as building his own house. 'There is,' he says, 'some of the same fitness in a man's building his own house, as there is in a bird's building its own nest. Who knows but if men constructed their dwellings with their own hands, and provided food for themselves and families, simply and honestly enough, the poetic faculty would be universally developed, as birds universally sing when they are thus engaged.' So, as he hewed his studs and rafters, he sang—if not as musically, at least quite as unintelligibly as any bird—

> 'Men say they know many things;
> But lo! they have taken wings —
> The arts and sciences,
> And a thousand appliances;
> The wind that blows
> Is all that anybody knows.'

As Mr. Thoreau squatted, he paid no rent; but the glass, iron-work, and other materials of his hut, which he could not make himself, cost twenty-eight dollars. The first year he lived in the woods, he earned, by day-labour, thirteen dollars, and the surplus produce of his beans he sold for twenty-three dollars; and as his food and clothing during that period cost him thirteen dollars only, he thus secured leisure, health, and independence, besides a comfortable house, as long as he chose to occupy it. Rice, Indian meal, beans, and molasses, were his principal articles of food. He sometimes caught a mess of fish; and the wood gratuitously supplied him with fuel for warmth and cooking. Work agreed with his constitution as little as 'doing good.' He tells us: 'I love a broad margin to my life. Sometimes in a summer morning, having taken my accustomed bath, I sat in my sunny doorway from sunrise till noon, rapt in reverie, amidst the pines, and hickories, and sumachs, in undisturbed solitude and stillness, while the birds sang around or flitted noiseless through the house, until by the sun falling in at my west window, or the noise of some traveller's wagon on the distant highway, I was reminded of the lapse of time. I grew in those seasons like corn in the night, and they were far better than any work of the hands would have been. They were not times subtracted from my life; but so much over and above my usual allowance. This was sheer idleness to my fellow-townsmen, no doubt; but if the birds and flowers had tried me by their standard, I should not have been found wanting.'

As he walked in the woods to see the birds and squirrels, so he sometimes walked in the village to see the men and boys. The village appeared to him as a great newsroom: its vitals were the grocery, the bar-room, the post office, and the bank; and as a necessary part of the machinery, it had a bell, a big gun, and a fire-engine. The houses were arranged to make the most of mankind, in lanes and fronting one another, so that every traveller had to run the gantlet, and every man, woman, and child might get a lick at him. But to one of his village visits there hangs a tale, which he shall tell himself: 'One afternoon, when I went to the village to get a shoe from the cobbler's, I was seized and put into jail, because I did not pay a tax to, or recognise the authority of, the state, which buys and sells men, women, and children, like cattle, at the door of its senate-house. I had gone down to the woods for other purposes. But wherever a man goes, men will pursue and paw him with their dirty institutions, and, if they can, constrain him to belong to their desperate odd-fellow society. It is true, I might have resisted forcibly, with more or less effect, might have run a *muck* against society; but I preferred that society should run a *muck* against me, it being the desperate party. However, I was released the next day, obtained my mended shoe, and returned to the woods in season to get my dinner of huckleberries on Fair Haven Hill.'

Mr. Thoreau failed in making any converts to his system; one person only, an idiotic pauper, from the village poor-house, expressed a wish to live as he did. An honest, hard-working, shiftless Irishman, however, seemed a more promising subject for conversion. This man worked for a farmer, turning up meadow, with a spade, for ten dollars an acre, with the use of the land and manure for one year, while a little broad-faced son worked cheerfully at his side. So as Mr. Thoreau relates: 'I tried to help him with my experience, telling him that he was one of my nearest neighbours, and that I, who looked like a loafer, was getting my living like himself; that I lived in a tight, light, and clean house, which hardly cost more than the annual rent of such a ruin as his commonly amounts to; and how, if he chose, he might in a month or two build himself a palace of his own; that I did not use tea, nor coffee, nor butter, nor milk, nor fresh meat, and so did not have to work to get them; again, as I did not work hard, I did not have to eat hard, and it cost me but a trifle for my food; but as he began with tea and coffee, and butter, and milk, and beef, he had to work hard to pay for them, and when he had worked hard, he had to eat hard again to repair the waste of his system. And so it was as broad as it was long—indeed, it was broader than it was long, for he was discontented, and wasted his life into the bargain. I told him that as he worked so hard, he required thick boots and stout clothing, which yet were soon soiled and worn out; but I wore light shoes and thin clothing, which cost not half so much; and in an hour or two, without labour, but as a recreation, I could catch as many fish as I should want for two days, or earn enough money to support me a week. If he and his family would live simply, they might all go a huckleberrying in the summer for their amusement.'

Puzzled, but not convinced, the Irishman and his 'greasy-faced wife' stared and scratched their heads. Such teaching must have sounded strangely to them, who had crossed the Atlantic to do their share of work in the world, and enjoy its reward in the form of tea, coffee, butter, and beef. Patrick, however, was silly enough to leave his work for that afternoon, and go a-fishing with the philosopher; but his 'derivative old-country mode of fishing disturbed only two fins.' So he wisely went back to his work the next morning, probably studying the proverb of his country which teaches, that 'hunger and ease is a dog's life;' and our author thus rather uncourteously dismisses him: 'With his horizon all his own, yet he a poor man, born to be poor, with his inherited Irish poverty, or poor life, his Adam's grandmother and boggy ways, not to rise in this world, he nor his posterity, till their wading, webbed, bog-trotting feet get *talaria* to their heels.'

Another Irishman, of a very different stamp, a squatter in the woods of Walden, might have proved a more facile subject for conversion; but he died just after making Mr. Thoreau's acquaintance. This man's name was Quoil; and when he did work, which was very seldom—for he liked work as little as Mr. Thoreau himself did—followed the occupation of a ditcher. Having, however, been a soldier in the British army, his American neighbours gave him the brevet rank of colonel. Colonel Quoil, Mr. Thoreau tells us, 'was a man of manners, like one who had seen the world, and capable of more civil speech than one could well attend to. He wore a greatcoat in midsummer, being affected with the trembling delirium, and his face was the colour of carmine. He died in the high-road. Before his house was pulled down, when his comrades avoided it as "an unlucky castle," I visited it. There lay his old clothes curled up by use, as if they were himself, on his raised plank-bed. His pipe lay broken on the hearth, instead of a bowl broken at the fountain. The last could never have been the symbol of his death, for he confessed that though he had heard of Brister's spring, he had never seen it; and soiled cards—diamonds, spades, and hearts—were scattered over the floor. One black chicken—black as night, and as silent—still went to roost in the apartment. In the rear, there was the dim outline of a garden, which had been planted, but had never received its first hoeing, though it was now harvest-time.'

The natural sights and sounds of the woods, as described by Mr. Thoreau, form much pleasanter reading than his vague and scarcely comprehensible social theories. He says: 'I had this advantage, at least, in my mode of life over those who were obliged to look abroad for amusement to society and the theatre, that my life itself was become my amusement, and never ceased to be novel. It was a drama of many scenes, and without an end. As I sit at my window this summer afternoon, hawks are circling about my clearing; the tantivy of wild pigeons, flying by twos and threes athwart my view, or perching restless on the white pine boughs behind my house, gives a voice to the air; a fish-hawk dimples the glassy surface of the pond, and brings up a fish; a mink steals out of the marsh before my door, and seizes a frog by the shore; the sedge is bending under the weight of the reed-birds flitting hither and thither; and for the last half-hour I have heard the rattle of railroad cars—now dying away, and then reviving like the beat of a partridge—conveying travellers from Boston to the country. At night,' he continues, 'when other birds are still, the screech-owl takes up the strain, like mourning women in their ancient *u-lu-lu*. Their dismal scream is truly Ben Jonsonian. "Wise midnight hags!" It is no honest and blunt *tu-whit tu-who* of the poets, but, without jesting, a most solemn graveyard ditty, the mutual consolations of suicide lovers remembering the pangs and the delights of supernal love in the infernal groves. Yet I love to hear their wailing, their doleful responses, trilled along the wood-side; reminding me sometimes of music and singing-birds, as if it were the dark and tearful side of music, the regrets and sighs that would fain be sung. They are the spirits, the low spirits and melancholy forebodings of fallen souls that once in human shape night-walked the earth and did the deeds of darkness, now expiating their sins with their wailing hymns or threnodies in the scenery of their transgressions. They give me a new sense of the variety and capacity of that nature which is our common dwelling. *Oh-o-o-o-o that I never had been bor-r-r-r-r-n!* sighs one on this side of the pond, and circles with the restlessness of despair to some new perch on the gray oaks. Then—*that I never had been bor-r-r-r-r-n!* echoes another on the further side with tremulous sincerity; and *bor-r-r-r-r-n!* comes faintly from far in the Lincoln woods. In the meanwhile, all the shore rang with the trump of bull-frogs, the sturdy spirits of ancient wine-bibbers and wassailers, still unrepentant, trying to sing a catch in their Stygian lake, though their voices have waxed hoarse and solemnly grave, mocking at mirth; and the wine has lost its flavour, and become only water to distend their paunches, and sweet intoxication never comes to drown the memory of the past, but mere saturation, and water-loggedness, and distension. The most aldermanic, with his chin upon a leaf, which serves for a napkin to his drooling chaps, under this northern shore quaffs a deep draught of the once scorned water, and passing round the cup with the ejaculation *tr-r-r-oonk, tr-r-r-oonk, tr-r-r-oonk!* and straightway comes over the water, from some distant cove, the same password repeated, where the next in seniority and girth has gulped down to his mark; and when this observance has made the circuit of the shores, then ejaculates the master of ceremonies, with satisfaction, *tr-r-r-oonk!* and each in its turn repeats the same, down to the least distended, leakiest, and flabbiest paunched, that there be no mistake; and then the bowl goes round again and again, until the sun disperses the morning mist, and only the patriarch is not under the pond, but vainly bellowing *troonk* from time to time, and pausing for a reply.'

Those were the summer sounds; in winter nights he heard the forlorn but melodious note of the hooting-owl, such a tone as the frozen earth would yield if struck with a suitable plectrum. 'I seldom,' he writes, 'opened my door in a winter evening without hearing it: *hoo hoo hoo, hoorer hoo,* sounded sonorously, and the first three syllables accented something like *how der do,* or sometimes *hoo hoo hoo* only. One night in the beginning of winter, before the pond froze over, about nine o'clock, I was startled by the loud *honking* of a goose, and stepping to the door, heard the sound of their wings, like a tempest in the woods, as a flock flew low over my house. They passed over the pond, seemingly deterred from settling by my light, their commodore *honking* all the while with a regular beat. Suddenly an unmistakable cat-owl, from very near me, with the most harsh and tremendous voice I ever heard from any inhabitant of the woods, responded at regular intervals to the goose, as if determined to expose and disgrace this intruder from Hudson Bay by exhibiting a greater compass and volume of voice in a native, and *boo hoo* him out of Concord horizon! What do you mean by alarming the citadel at this time of night consecrated to me? Do you think I am ever caught napping at such an hour, and that I have not got lungs and larynx as well as yourself? *Boo-hoo, boo-hoo, boo-hoo.* It was one of the most thrilling discords I ever heard. And yet, to a discriminating ear, there were in it the elements of a concord such as these plains never saw nor heard.'

'Sometimes,' Mr. Thoreau continues, 'I heard the foxes, as they ranged over the snow-crust, in moon-light nights, in search of a partridge or other game, barking raggedly and demoniacally like forest-dogs, as if labouring with some anxiety, or seeking expression, struggling for light, and to be dogs outright, and run freely in the streets; for if we take the ages into our account, may there not be a civilisation going on amoung brutes as well as men? They seemed to me to be rudimental burrowing men, still standing on their defence, awaiting their transformation. Sometimes one came near to my window, attracted by my light, barked a vulpine curse at me, and then retreated.'

Mr. Thoreau went to the woods, because he wished to live deliberately, to front only the essential facts of life, and see whether he could learn what it had to teach; so that when he came to die, he might not discover that he had not lived. After supporting animal and intellectual life for two years, at the cost of thirteen dollars per annum, he 'left the woods for as good a reason as he went there.' It seemed to him that he had several more lives to live, so he could not spare any more time for that particular one. He learned however, by his experiment, 'that it is not necessary a man should earn his living by the sweat of his brow; and to maintain one's self on this earth is not a hardship but a pastime, if we will live simply and wisely. Moreover, if a man advances confidently in the direction of his dreams, and endeavours to live the life which he has imagined, he will meet with a success unexpected in common hours. In proportion as he simplifies his life, the laws of the universe will appear less complex, and solitude will not be solitude, nor poverty poverty, nor weakness weakness.'

Who is it, we have more than once mentally inquired, when penning the preceding sketch, that Mr. Thoreau reminds us of? Surely it cannot be—yes, it is—no other than his renowned compatriot Barnum. As homespun, beans, and water differ from fine linen, turtle, and champagne, so do the two men differ in tastes, habits, disposition, and culture; yet we cannot think of the one without an ideal association of the other. In one respect only do they seem to agree—both have an antipathy to hard work; but while one prefers diminishing his wants, the other, increasing them, invents extraordinary schemes for their gratification. If Barnum's autobiography be a bane, Thoreau's woodland experiences may be received as its antidote; but, unfortunately, the former musters its readers by tens of thousands, the latter probably in hundreds only. It is to be hoped, however—though all of us have a reasonable predilection for beef, pudding, and the society of our fellow-creatures—that there are few readers of this Journal who would not prefer eating beans in the woods with Thoreau to living on the fat of the earth, in the best show in all Vanity Fair, with Barnum.

[1862]

When Thoreau died in 1862, his friend and neighbor Ralph Waldo Emerson was asked to preach the funeral sermon. This eulogy was later revised and published as an essay. Perhaps no other single work had such a wide influence on the reputation of Thoreau. Written with every intention of honoring a departed friend, it had a most devastating effect on his fame. Emerson idealized Thoreau as a Stoic. When he came to edit Thoreau's letters in 1865, he cut from them every line that showed his warm, friendly personality, and emphasized his philosophical aloofness. The same touch can be discerned here. Thoreau is portrayed essentially in the negative, as one who found it easier to say No than Yes. Emerson created the concept of Thoreau as an unfeeling Stoic. Paradoxically enough, it was Emerson's son Edward who later most emphatically protested this picture of Thoreau and who helped in his centennial tribute, Henry Thoreau as Remembered by a Young Friend, *to rehabilitate him as the most vital of all the Transcendentalists.*

THOREAU

BY RALPH WALDO EMERSON

Henry David Thoreau was the last male descendant of a French ancestor who came to this country from the Isle of Guernsey. His character exhibited occasional traits drawn from this blood, in singular combination with a very strong Saxon genius.

He was born in Concord, Massachusetts, on the 12th of July, 1817. He was graduated at Harvard College in 1837, but without any literary distinction. An iconoclast in literature, he seldom

---

From *Atlantic Monthly,* X (August, 1862), 239-49. A long series of quotations has been omitted.

thanked colleges for their service to him, holding them in small esteem, whilst yet his debt to them was important. After leaving the University, he joined his brother in teaching a private school, which he soon renounced. His father was a manufacturer of lead-pencils, and Henry applied himself for a time to this craft, believing he could make a better pencil than was in use then. After completing his experiments, he exhibited his work to chemists and artists in Boston, and having obtained their certificates to its excellence and to its equality with the best London manufacture, he returned home contented. His friends congratulated him that he had now opened his way to fortune. But he replied, that he should never make another pencil. "Why should I? I would not do again what I have done once." He resumed his endless walks and miscellaneous studies, making every day some new acquaintance with Nature, though as yet never speaking of zoology or botany, since, though very studious of natural facts, he was incurious of technical and textual science.

At this time, a strong, healthy youth, fresh from college, whilst all his companions were choosing their profession, or eager to begin some lucrative employment, it was inevitable that his thoughts should be exercised on the same question, and it required rare decision to refuse all the accustomed paths and keep his solitary freedom at the cost of disappointing the natural expectations of his family and friends: all the more difficult that he had a perfect probity, was exact in securing his own independence, and in holding every man to the like duty. But Thoreau never faltered. He was a born protestant. He declined to give up his large ambition of knowledge and action for any narrow craft or profession, aiming at a much more comprehensive calling, the art of living well. If he slighted and defied the opinions of others, it was only that he was more intent to reconcile his practice with his own belief. Never idle or self-indulgent, he preferred, when he wanted money, earning it by some piece of manual labor agreeable to him, as building a boat or a fence, planting, grafting, surveying, or other short work, to any long engagements. With his hardy habits and few wants, his skill in wood-craft, and his powerful arithmetic, he was very competent to live in any part of the world. It would cost him less time to supply his wants than another. He was therefore secure of his leisure.

A·natural skill for mensuration, growing out of his mathematical knowledge and his habit of ascertaining the measures and distances of objects which interested him, the size of trees, the depth and extent of ponds and rivers, the height of mountains, and the air-line distance of his favorite summits,—this, and his intimate knowledge of the territory about Concord, made him drift into the profession of land-surveyor. It had the advantage for him that it led him continually into new and secluded grounds, and helped his studies of Nature. His accuracy and skill in this work were readily appreciated, and he found all the employment he wanted.

He could easily solve the problems of the surveyor, but he was daily beset with graver questions, which he manfullv confronted. He interrogated every custom, and wished to settle all his practice on an ideal foundation. He was a protestant *á outrance,* and few lives contain so many renunciations. He was bred to no profession; he never married; he lived alone; he never went to church; he never voted; he refused to pay a tax to the State; he ate no flesh, he drank no wine, he never knew the use of tobacco; and, though a naturalist, he used neither trap nor gun. He chose, wisely no doubt, for himself, to be the bachelor of thought and Nature. He had no talent for wealth, and knew how to be poor without the least hint of squalor or inelegance. Perhaps he fell into his way of living without forecasting it much, but approved it with later wisdom. "I am often reminded," he wrote in his journal, "that if I had bestowed on me the wealth of Croesus, my aims must be still the same, and my means essentially the same." He had no temptations to fight against,—no appetites, no passions, no taste for elegant trifles. A fine house, dress, the manners and talk of highly cultivated people were all thrown away on him. He much preferred a good Indian, and considered these refinements as impediments to conversation, wishing to meet his companion on the simplest terms. He declined invitations to dinner-parties, because there each was in every one's way, and he could not meet the individuals to any purpose. "They make their pride," he said, "in making their dinner cost much; I make my pride in making my dinner cost little." When asked at table what dish he preferred, he answered, "The nearest." He did not like the taste of wine, and never had a vice in his life. He said,—"I have a faint recollection of pleasure derived from smoking dried lily-stems, before I was a man. I had commonly a supply of these. I have never smoked anything more noxious."

He chose to be rich by making his wants few, and supplying them himself. In his travels, he used the railroad only to get over so much country as was unimportant to the present purpose, walking hundreds of miles, avoiding taverns, buying a lodging in farmers' and fishermen's houses, as cheaper, and more agreeable to him, and because there he could better find the men and the information he wanted.

There was somewhat military in his nature, not to be subdued, always manly and able, but rarely tender, as if he did not feel himself except in opposition. He wanted a fallacy to expose, a blunder to pillory, I may say required a little sense of victory, a roll of the drum, to call his powers into full exercise. It cost him nothing to say No; indeed he found it much easier than to say Yes. It seemed as if his first instinct on hearing a proposition was to controvert it, so impatient was he of the limitations of our daily thought. This habit, of course, is a little chilling to the social affections; and though the companion would in the end acquit him of any malice or untruth, yet it mars conversation. Hence, no equal companion stood in affectionate relations with one so pure and guileless. "I love Henry," said one of his friends, "but I cannot like him; and as for taking his arm, I should as soon think of taking the arm of an elm-tree."

Yet, hermit and stoic as he was, he was really fond of sympathy, and threw himself heartily and childlike into the company of young people whom he loved, and whom he delighted to entertain, as he only could, with the varied and endless anecdotes of his experiences by field and river: and he was always ready to lead a huckleberry-party or a search for chestnuts or grapes. Talking, one day, of a public discourse, Henry remarked, that whatever succeeded with the audience was bad. I said, "Who would not like to write something which all can read, like Robinson Crusoe? and who does not see with regret that his page is not solid with a right materialistic treatment, which delights everybody?" Henry objected, of course, and vaunted the better lectures which reached only a few persons. But, at supper, a young girl, understanding that he was to lecture at the Lyceum, sharply asked him, "Whether his lecture would be a nice, interesting story, such as she wished to hear, or whether it was one of those old philosophical things that she did not care about." Henry turned to her, and bethought himself, and, I saw, was trying to believe that he had matter that might fit her and her brother who were to sit up and go to the lecture, if it was a good one for them.

He was a speaker and actor of the truth, born such, and was ever running into dramatic situations from this cause. In any circumstance it interested all bystanders to know what part Henry would take, and what he would say; and he did not disappoint expectation, but used an original judgment on each emergency. In 1845 he built himself a small framed house on the shores of Walden Pond, and lived there two years alone, a life of labor and study. This action was quite native and fit for him. No one who knew him would tax him with affectation. He was more unlike his neighbors in his thought than in his action. As soon as he had exhausted the advantages of that solitude, he abandoned it. In 1847, not approving some uses to which the public expenditure was applied, he refused to pay his town tax, and was put in jail. A friend paid the tax for him, and he was released. The like annoyance was threatened the next year. But, as his friends paid the tax, notwithstanding his protest, I believe he ceased to resist. No opposition or ridicule had any weight with him. He coldly and fully stated his opinion without affecting to believe that it was the opinion of the company. It was of no consequence if every one present held the opposite opinion. On one occasion he went to the University Library to procure some books. The librarian refused to lend them. Mr. Thoreau repaired to the President, who stated to him the rules and usages, which permitted the loan of books to resident graduates, to clergymen who were alumni, and to some others resident within a circle of ten miles' radius from the College. Mr. Thoreau explained to the President that the railroad had destroyed the old scale of distances,—that the library was useless, yes, and President and College useless, on the terms of his rules,—that the one benefit he owed to the College was its library,—that, at this moment, not only his want of books was imperative but he wanted a large number of books, and assured him that he, Thoreau, and not the librarian, was the proper custodian of these. In short, the President found the petitioner so formidable, and the rules getting to look so ridiculous, that he ended by giving him a privilege which in his hands proved unlimited thereafter.

No truer American existed than Thoreau. His preference of his country and condition was genuine, and his aversation from English and European manners and tastes almost reached contempt. He listened impatiently to news or *bonmots* gleaned from London circles; and though he tried to be civil, these andecdotes fatigued him. The men were all imitating each other, and on a small mould. Why can they not live as far apart as possible, and each be a man by himself? What he sought was the most energetic nature; and he wished to go to Oregon, not to London. "In every part of Great Britain," he wrote in his diary, "are discovered traces of the Romans, their funereal urns, their camps, their roads, their dwellings. But New England, at least, is not based on any Roman ruins. We have not to lay the foundations of our houses on the ashes of a former civilization."

But, idealist as he was, standing for abolition of slavery, abolition of tariffs, almost for abolition of government, it is needless to say he found himself not only unrepresented in actual politics, but almost equally opposed to every class of reformers. Yet he paid the tribute of his uniform respect to the Anti-Slavery party. One man, whose personal acquaintance he had formed, he honored with exceptional regard. Before the first friendly word had been spoken for Captain John Brown, he sent notices to most houses in Concord that he would speak in a public hall on the condition and character of John Brown, on Sunday evening, and invited all people to come. The Republican Committee, the Abolitionist Committee, sent him word that it was premature and not advisable. He replied,—"I did not send to you for advice, but to announce that I am to speak." The hall was filled at an early hour by people of all parties, and his earnest eulogy of the hero was heard by all respectfuly, by many with a sympathy that surprised themselves.

It was said of Plotinus that he was ashamed of his body, and 'tis very likely he had good reason for it,—that his body was a bad servant, and he had not skill in dealing with the material world, as happens often to men of abstract intellect. But Mr. Thoreau was equipped with a most adapted and serviceable body. He was of short stature, firmly built, of light complexion, with strong, serious blue eyes, and a grave aspect,—his face covered in the late years with a becoming beard. His senses were acute, his frame well-knit and hardy, his hands strong and skillful in the use of tools. And there was a wonderful fitness of body and mind. He could pace sixteen rods more accurately than another man could measure them with rod and chain. He could find his path in the woods at night, he said, better by his feet than his eyes. He could estimate the measure of a tree very well by his eye; he could estimate the weight of a calf or a pig, like a dealer. From a box containing a bushel or more of loose pencils, he could take up with his hands fast enough just a dozen pencils at every grasp. He was a good swimmer, runner, skater, boatman, and would probably outwalk most countrymen in a day's journey. And the relation of body to mind was still finer than we have indicated. He said he wanted every stride his legs made. The length of his walk uniformly made the length of his writing. If shut up in the house, he did not write at all.

He had a strong common-sense, like that which Rose Flammock the weaver's daughter in Scott's romance commends in her father, as resembling a yardstick, which, whilst it measures dowlas and diaper, can equally well measure tapestry and cloth of gold. He had always a new resource. When I was planting forest trees, and had procured half a peck of acorns, he said that only a small portion of them would be sound, and proceeded to examine them and select the sound ones. But finding this took time, he said, "I think if you put them all into water the good ones will sink;" which experiment we tried with success. He could plan a garden or a house or a barn; would have been competent to lead a "Pacific Exploring Expedition;" could give judicious counsel in the gravest private or public affairs.

He lived for the day, not cumbered and mortified by his memory. If he brought you yesterday a new proposition, he would bring you today another not less revolutionary. A very industrious man, and setting, like all highly organized men, a high value on his time, he seemed the only man of leisure in town, always ready for any excursion that promised well, or for conversation prolonged into late hours. His trenchant sense was never stopped by his rules of daily prudence, but was always up to the new occasion. He liked and used the simplest food, yet, when some one urged a vegetable diet, Thoreau thought all diets a very small matter, saying that "the man who shoots the buffalo lives better than the man who boards at the Graham House." He said,—"You can sleep near the railroad, and never be disturbed: Nature knows very well what sounds are worth attending to, and has made up her mind not to hear the railroad-whistle. But things respect the devout mind, and a mental ectasy was never interrupted." He noted what repeatedly befell him, that, after receiving from a distance a rare plant, he would presently find the same in his own haunts. And those pieces of luck which happen only to good players happened to him. One day, walking with a stranger, who inquired where Indian arrow-heads could be found, he replied, "Everywhere," and, stooping forward, picked one on the instant from the ground. At Mount Washington, in Tuckerman's Ravine, Thoreau had a bad fall, and sprained his foot. As he was in the act of getting up from his fall, he saw for the first time the leaves of the *Arnica mollis*.

His robust common sense, armed with stout hands, keen perceptions and strong will, cannot yet account for the superiority

which shone in his simple and hidden life. I must add the cardinal
fact, that there was an excellent wisdom in him, proper to a rare
class of men, which showed him the material world as a means and
symbol. This discovery, which sometimes yields to poets a certain
casual and interrupted light, serving for the ornament of their
writing, was in him an unsleeping insight; and whatever faults or
obstructions of temperament might cloud it, he was not disobe-
dient to the heavenly vision. In his youth, he said, one day, "The
other world is all my art; my pencils will draw no other; my jack-
knife will cut nothing else; I do not use it as a means." This was
the muse and genius that ruled his opinions, conversation, studies,
work and course of life. This made him a searching judge of men.
At first glance he measured his companion, and, though insensible
to some fine traits of culture, could very well report his weight
and calibre. And this made the impression of genius which his
conversation sometimes gave.

He understood the matter in hand at a glance, and saw the limitations and poverty of those he talked with, so that nothing seemed
concealed from such terrible eyes. I have repeatedly known young
men of sensibility converted in a moment to the belief that this
was the man they were in search of, the man of men, who could
tell them all they should do. His own dealing with them was never
affectionate, but superior, didactic, scorning their petty ways,—
very slowly conceding, or not conceding at all, the promise of his
society at their houses, or even at his own. "Would he not walk
with them?" "He did not know. There was nothing so important
to him as his walk; he had no walks to throw away on company."
Visits were offered him from respectful parties, but he declined
them. Admiring friends offered to carry him at their own cost to
the Yellowstone River,—to the West Indies,—to South America.
But though nothing could be more grave or considered than his
refusals, they remind one, in quite new relations, of that fop
Brummell's reply to the gentleman who offered him his carriage in
a shower, "But where will *you* ride, then?"—and what accusing
silences, and what searching and irresistible speeches, battering
down all defenses, his companions can remember!

Mr. Thoreau dedicated his genius with such entire love to the fields, hills and waters of his native town, that he made them known and interesting to all reading Americans, and to people over the sea. The river on whose banks he was born and died he knew from its springs to its confluence with the Merrimack. He had made summer and winter observations on it for many years, and at every hour of the day and night. The result of the recent survey of the Water Commissioners appointed by the State of Massachusetts he had reached by his private experiments, several years earlier. Every fact which occurs in the bed, on the banks, or in the air over it; the fishes, and their spawning and nests, their manners, their food; the shad-flies which fill the air on a certain evening once a year, and which are snapped at by the fishes so ravenously that many of these die of repletion; the conical heaps of small stones on the river-shallows, the huge nests of small fishes, one of which will sometimes overfill a cart; the birds which frequent the stream, heron, duck, sheldrake, loon, osprey; the snake, muskrat, otter, woodchuck and fox, on the banks; the turtle, frog, hyla, and cricket, which make the banks vocal,— were all known to him, and, as it were, townsmen and fellow-creatures; so that he felt an absurdity or violence in any narrative of one of these by itself apart, and still more of its dimensions on an inch-rule, or in the exhibition of its skeleton, or the specimen of a squirrel or a bird in brandy. He liked to speak of the manners of the river, as itself a lawful creature, yet with exactness, and always to an observed fact. As he knew the river, so the ponds in this region.

One of the weapons he used, more important to him than microscope or alcohol-receiver to other investigators, was a whim which grew on him by indulgence, yet appeared in gravest statement, namely, of extolling his own town and neighborhood as the most favored centre for natural observation. He remarked that the Flora of Massachusetts embraced almost all the important plants of America,—most of the oaks, most of the willows, the best pines, the ash, the maple, the beech, the nuts. He returned Kane's "Arctic Voyage" to a friend of whom he had borrowed it, with the remark, that "Most of the phenomena noted might be observed in Concord." He seemed a little envious of the Pole, for the coincident sunrise and sunset, or five minutes' day after six months: a splendid fact, which Annursnuc had never afforded him. He found red snow in one of his walks, and told me that he expected to find yet the *Victoria regia* in Concord. He was the attorney of the indigenous plants, and owned to a preference of the weeds to the imported plants as of the Indian to the civilized man, and noticed, with pleasure, that the willow bean-poles of his neighbor had grown more than his beans. "See these weeds," he said, "which have been hoed at by a million farmers all spring and summer, and yet have prevailed, and just now come out triumphant over all lanes, pastures, fields and gardens, such is their vigor. We have insulted them with low names, too,—as Pigweed, Wormwood, Chickweed, Shad-blossom." He says, "They have brave names, too,—Ambrosia, Stellaria, Amelanchier, Amaranth, etc."

I think his fancy for referring everything to the meridian of Concord did not grow out of any ignorance or depreciation of other longitudes or latitudes, but was rather a playful expression of his conviction of the indifferency of all places, and that the best place for each is where he stands. He expressed it once in this wise:—"I think nothing is to be hoped from you, if this bit of mould under your feet is not sweeter to you to eat than any other in this world, or in any world."

The other weapon with which he conquered all obstacles in science was patience. He knew how to sit immovable, a part of the rock he rested on, until the bird, the reptile, the fish, which had retired from him, should come back and resume its habits, nay, moved by curiosity, should come to him and watch him.

It was a pleasure and a privilege to walk with him. He knew the country like a fox or a bird, and passed through it as freely by paths of his own. He knew every track in the snow or on the ground, and what creature had taken this path before him. One must submit abjectly to such a guide, and the reward was great. Under his arm he carried an old music-book to press plants; in his pocket, his diary and pencil, a spy-glass for birds, miscroscope, jack-knife, and twine. He wore a straw hat, stout shoes, strong gray trousers, to brave scrub-oaks and smilax, and to climb a tree for a hawk's or a squirrel's nest. He waded into the pool for the water-plants, and his strong legs were no insignificant part of his armor. On the day I speak of he looked for the Menyanthes, detected it across the wide pool, and, on examination of the florets, decided that it had been in flower five days. He drew out of his breast-pocket his diary, and read the names of all the plants that should bloom on this day, whereof he kept account as a banker when his notes fall due. The Cypripedium not due till to-morrow. He thought that, if waked up from a trance, in this swamp, he could tell by the plants what time of the year it was within two days. The redstart was flying about, and presently the fine gros-beaks, whose brilliant scarlet "makes the rash gazer wipe his eye," and whose fine clear note Thoreau compared to that of a tanager which has got rid of its hoarseness. Presently he heard a note which he called that of the night-warbler, a bird he had never identified, had been in search of twelve years, which al-ways, when he saw it was in the act of diving down into a tree or bush, and which it was vain to seek; the only bird which sings indifferently by night and by day. I told him he must beware of finding and booking it, lest life should have nothing more to show him. He said, "What you seek in vain for, half your life, one day you come full upon, all the family at dinner. You seek it like a dream, and as soon as you find it you become its prey."

His interest in the flower or the bird lay very deep in his mind, was connected with Nature,—and the meaning of Nature was never attempted to be defined by him. He would not offer a memoir of his observations to the Natural History Society. "Why should I? To detach the description from its connections in my mind would make it no longer true or valuable to me: and they do not wish what belongs to it." His power of observation seemed to indicate additional senses. He saw as with microscope, heard as with ear-trumpet, and his memory was a photographic register of all he saw and heard. And yet none knew better than he that it is not the fact that imports, but the impression or effect of the fact on your mind. Every fact lay in glory in his mind, a type of the order and beauty of the whole.

His determination on Natural History was organic. He confessed that he sometimes felt like a hound or a panther, and, if born among Indians, would have been a fell hunter. But, restrained by his Massachusetts culture, he played out the game in this mild form of botany and ichthyology. His intimacy with animals suggested what Thomas Fuller records of Butler the apiologist, that "either he had told the bees things or the bees had told him." Snakes coiled round his leg; the fishes swam into his hand, and he took them out of the water; he pulled the woodchuck out of its hole by the tail and took the foxes under his protection from the hunters. Our naturalist had perfect magnanimity; he had no secrets: he would carry you to the heron's haunt, or even to his most prized botanical swamp,—possibly knowing that you could never find it again, yet willing to take his risks.

No college ever offered him a diploma, or a professor's chair; no academy made him its corresponding secretary, its discoverer, or even its member. Perhaps these learned bodies feared the satire of his presence. Yet so much knowledge of Nature's secret and genius few others possessed; none in a more large and religious synthesis. For not a particle of respect had he to the opinions of any man or body of men, but homage solely to the truth itself; and as he discovered everywhere among doctors some leaning of courtesy, it discredited them. He grew to be revered and admired by his townsmen, who had at first known him only as an oddity. The farmers who employed him as a surveyor soon discovered his rare accuracy and skill, his knowledge of their lands, of trees, of birds, of Indian remains and the like, which enabled him to tell every farmer more than he knew before of his own farm; so that he began to feel a little as if Mr. Thoreau had better rights in his land than he. They felt, too, the superiority of character which addressed all men with a native authority.

Indian relics abound in Concord,—arrow-heads, stone chisels, pestles, and fragments of pottery; and on the river-bank, large heaps of clam-shells and ashes mark spots which the savages frequented. These, and every circumstance touching the Indian, were important in his eyes. His visits to Maine were chiefly for love of the Indian. He had the satisfaction of seeing the manufacture of the bark-canoe, as well as of trying his hand in its management on the rapids. He was inquisitive about the making of the stone arrow-head, and in his last days charged a youth setting out for the Rocky Mountains to find an Indian who could tell him that: "It was well worth a visit to California to learn it." Occasionally, a small party of Penobscot Indians would visit Concord, and pitch their tents for a few weeks in summer on the river-bank. He failed not to make acquaintance with the best of them; though he well knew that asking questions of Indians is like catechizing beavers and rabbits. In his last visit to Maine he had great satisfaction from Joseph Polis, an intelligent Indian of Oldtown, who was his guide for some weeks.

He was equally interested in every natural fact. The depth of his perception found likeness of law throughout Nature, and I know not any genius who so swiftly inferred universal law from the single fact. He was no pedant of a department. His eye was open to beauty, and his ear to music. He found these, not in rare conditions, but wheresoever he went. He thought the best of music was in single strains; and he found poetic suggestion in the humming of the telegraph-wire.

His poetry might be bad or good; he no doubt wanted a lyric facility and technical skill, but he had the source of poetry in his spiritual perception. He was a good reader and critic, and his judgment on poetry was to the ground of it. He could not be deceived as to the presence or absence of the poetic element in any composition, and his thirst for this made him negligent and perhaps scornful of superficial graces. He would pass by many delicate rhythms, but he would have detected every live stanza or line in a volume, and knew very well where to find an equal poetic charm in prose. He was so enamored of the spiritual beauty that he held all actual written poems in very light esteem in the comparison. He admired Æschylus and Pindar; but, when some one was commending them, he said that Æschylus and the Greeks, in describing Apollo and Orpheus, had given no song, or no good one. "They ought not to have moved trees, but to have chanted to the gods such a hymn as would have sung all their old ideas out of their heads, and new ones in." His own verses are often rude and defective. The gold does not yet run pure, is drossy and crude. The thyme and marjoram are not yet honey. But if he want lyric fineness and technical merits, if he have not the poetic temperament, he never lacks the casual thought, showing that his genius was better than his talent. He knew the worth of the Imagination for the uplifting and consolation of human life, and liked to throw every thought into a symbol. The fact you tell is of no value, but only the impression. For this reason his presence was poetic, always piqued the curiosity to know more deeply the secrets of his mind. He had many reserves, an unwillingness to exhibit to profane eyes what was still sacred in his own, and knew well how to throw a poetic veil over his experience. All readers of "Walden" will remember his mythical record of his disappointments:—

"I long ago lost a hound, a bay horse and a turtle-dove, and am still on their trail. Many are the travellers I have spoken concerning them, describing their tracks, and what calls they answered to. I have met one or two who have heard the hound, and the tramp of the horse, and even seen the dove disappear behind a cloud; and they seemed as anxious to recover them as if they had lost them them-selves."

His riddles were worth the reading, and I confide that if at any time I do not understand the expression, it is yet just. Such was the wealth of his truth that it was not worth his while to use words in vain. His poem entitled "Sympathy" reveals the tenderness under that triple steel of stoicism, and the intellectual subtility it could animate. His classic poem on "Smoke" suggests Simonides, but is better than any poem of Simonides. His biography is in his verses. His habitual thought makes all his poetry a hymn to the Cause of causes, the Spirit which vivifies and controls his own:—

> "I hearing get, who had but ears,
> And sight, who had but eyes before;
> I moments live, who lived but years,
> And truth discern, who knew but learning's lore."

And still more in these religious lines:—

> "Now chiefly is my natal hour
> And only now my prime of life;
> I will not doubt the love untold,
> Which not my worth nor want have bought,
> Which wooed me young, and wooes me old,
> And to this evening hath me brought."

Whilst he used in his writings a certain petulance of remark in reference to churches or churchmen, he was a person of a rare, tender and absolute religion, a person incapable of any profanation, by act or by thought. Of course, the same isolation which belonged to his original thinking and living detached him from the social religious forms. This is neither to be censured nor regretted. Aristotle long ago explained it, when he said, "One who surpasses his fellow-citizens in virtue is no longer a part of the city. Their law is not for him, since he is a law to himself."

Thoreau was sincerity itself, and might fortify the convictions of prophets in the ethical laws by his holy living. It was an affirmative experience which refused to be set aside. A truth-speaker he, capable of the most deep and strict conversation; a physician to the wounds of any soul; a friend, knowing not only the secret of friendship, but almost worshipped by those few persons who resorted to him as their confessor and prophet, and knew the deep value of his mind and great heart. He thought that without religion or devotion of some kind nothing great was ever accomplished: and he thought that the bigoted sectarian had better bear this in mind.

His virtues, of course, sometimes ran into extremes. It was easy to trace to the inexorable demand on all for exact truth that austerity which made this willing hermit more solitary even than he wished. Himself of a perfect probity, he required not less of others. He had a disgust at crime, and no worldly success would cover it. He detected paltering as readily in dignified and prosperous persons as in beggars, and with equal scorn. Such dangerous frankness was in his dealing that his admirers called him "that terrible Thoreau," as if he spoke when silent, and was still present when he had departed. I think the severity of his ideal interfered to deprive him of a healthy sufficiency of human society.

The habit of a realist to find things the reverse of their appearance inclined him to put every statement in a paradox. A certain habit of antagonism defaced his earlier writings,—a trick of rhetoric not quite outgrown in his later, of substituting for the obvious word and thought its diametrical opposite. He praised wild mountains and winter forests for their domestic air, in snow and ice he would find sultriness, and commended the wilderness for resembling Rome and Paris. "It was so dry, that you might call it wet."

The tendency to magnify the moment, to read all the laws of Nature in the one object or one combination under your eye, is of course comic to those who do not share the philosopher's perception of identity. To him there was no such thing as size. The pond was a small ocean; the Atlantic, a large Walden Pond. He referred every minute fact to cosmical laws. Though he meant to be just, he seemed haunted by a certain chronic assumption that the science of the day pretended completeness, and he had just found out that the *savans* had neglected to discriminate a particular botanical variety, had failed to describe the seeds or count the sepals. "That is to say," we replied, "the blockheads were not born in Concord; but who said they were? It was their unspeakable misfortune to be born in London, or Paris, or Rome; but, poor fellows, they did what they could, considering that they never saw Bateman's Pond, or Nine-Acre Corner, or Becky Stow's Swamp; besides, what were you sent into the world for, but to add this observation?"

Had his genius been only contemplative, he had been fitted to his life, but with his energy and practical ability he seemed born for great enterprise and for command; and I so much regret the loss of his rare powers of action, that I cannot help counting it a fault in him that he had no ambition. Wanting this, instead of engineering for all America, he was the captain of a huckleberry-party. Pounding beans is good to the end of pounding empires one of these days; but if, at the end of years, it is still only beans! But these foibles, real or apparent, were fast vanishing in the incessant growth of a spirit so robust and wise, and which effaced its defeats with new triumphs. His study of Nature was a perpetual ornament to him, and inspired his friends with curiosity to see the world through his eyes, and to hear his adventures. They possessed every kind of interest.

He had many elegancies of his own, whilst he scoffed at conventional elegance. Thus, he could not bear to hear the sound of his own steps, the grit of gravel; and therefore never willingly walked in the road, but in the grass, on mountains and in woods. His senses were acute, and he remarked that by night every dwelling-house gives out bad air, like a slaughter-house. He liked the pure fragrance of melilot. He honored certain plants with special regard, and, over all, the pond-lily,—then, the gentian, and the *Mikania scandens,* and "life-everlasting," and a bass-tree which he visited every year when it bloomed, in the middle of July. He thought the scent a more oracular inquisition than the sight,—more oracular and trustworthy. The scent, of course, reveals what is concealed from the other senses. By it he detected earthiness. He delighted in echoes, and said they were almost the only kind of kindred voices that he heard. He loved Nature so well, was so happy in her solitude, that he became very jealous of cities, the sad work which their refinements and artifices made with man and his dwelling. The axe was always destroying his forest. "Thank God," he said, "they cannot cut down the clouds!" "All kinds of figures are drawn on the blue ground with this fibrous white paint." . . .

There is a flower known to botanists, one of the same genus with our summer plant called "Life-Everlasting," a *Gnaphalium* like that, which grows on the most inaccessible cliffs of the Tyrolese mountains, where the chamois dare hardly venture, and which the hunter, tempted by its beauty, and by his love (for it is immensely valued by the Swiss maidens), climbs the cliffs to gather, and is sometimes found dead at the foot, with the flower in his hand. It is called by botanists the *Gnaphalium leontopodium,* but by the Swiss *Edelweisse,* which signifies *Noble Purity.* Thoreau seemed to me living in the hope to gather this plant, which belonged to him of right. The scale on which his studies proceeded was so large as to require longevity, and we were the less prepared for his sudden disappearance. The country knows not yet, or in the least part, how great a son it has lost. It seems an injury that he should leave in the midst his broken task which none else can finish, a kind of indignity to so noble a soul that he should depart out of Nature before yet he has been really shown to his peers for what he is. But he, at least, is content. His soul was made for the noblest society; he had in a short life exhausted the capabilities of this world; wherever there is knowledge, wherever there is virtue, wherever there is beauty, he will find a home.

[1865]

Shortly after Thoreau's death, his sister Sophia and friends Ralph Waldo Emerson and William Ellery Channing gathered together many of his uncollected and unpublished works and issued them in a series of volumes. Higginson, a Unitarian minister, minor Transcendentalist, and friend of Thoreau, wrote reviews of several of these works. The essay on Cape Cod *continues Emerson's Stoic theme, but in later writings Higginson was to emphasize Thoreau's friendliness and good nature.*

CAPE COD

A Review

BY THOMAS WENTWORTH HIGGINSON

Cape Cod is photographed at last, for Thoreau has been there. Day by day, with his stout pedestrian shoes, he plodded along that level beach,—the eternal ocean on one side, and human existence reduced to its simplest elements on the other,—and he pitilessly weighing each. His mental processes never impress one with opulence and luxuriance, but rather with a certain sublime tenacity, which extracts nutriment from the most barren soil. He is therefore admirably matched against Cape Cod; and though his books on softer aspects of Nature may have a mellower charm, there is none in which the very absence of mellowness can so well pass for an added merit.

No doubt there are passages which err upon the side of bareness. Cape Cod itself certainly errs that way, and so often does our author; and when they are combined, the result of desiccation

Atlantic Monthly, XV (March, 1865), 381.

is sometimes astounding. But so much the truer the picture. If Vedder's "Lair of the Sea-Serpent" had the rank verdure of the "Heart of the Andes," the kraken would still be as unimpressive on canvas as in the newspapers. No one ever dared to exhibit Cape Cod "long, and lank, and brown" enough before, and hence the value of the book. For those who insist on *Chlorophylle,* is there not "Azarian"? If the dear public will tolerate neither the presence of color in a picture, nor its absence, it is hard to suit.

Yet it is worth remembering, that Thoreau's one perfect poem,— and one of the most perfect in American literature,—"My life is like a stroll upon the beach," must have been suggested by Cape Cod or some kindred locality. And it is not the savage grandeur of the sea alone, but its delicate loveliness and its ever-budding life, which will be found recorded forever in some of these wondrous pages, intermixed with the statistics of fish-flakes and the annals of old men's diseases.

But in his stern realism, the author employs what he himself calls "Panurgic" plainness of speech, and deals with the horrors of the seashore as composedly as with its pearls. His descriptions of the memorials of shipwrecks, for instance, would be simply repulsive, but that his very dryness has a sort of disinfectant quality, like the air of California, where things the most loathsome may lie around us without making the air impure.

He shows his wonted formidable accuracy all through these pages, and the critic feels a sense of bewildered exultation in detecting him even in a slip of the pen, —as when in the note on page 228 he gives to the town of Rockport, on Cape Ann, the erroneous name of Rockland. After this discovery, one may dare to wonder at his finding a novelty in the "Upland Plover," and naming it among the birds not heard in the interior of the State, when he might be supposed to have observed it, in summer, near Mount Wachusett, where its wail adds so much, by day or night, to the wildness of the scenery. Yet by the triviality of these our criticisms one may measure the astonishing excellence of his books.

This wondrous eye and hand have passed away, and left no equal and no second. Everything which Thoreau wrote has this peculiar value, that no other observing powers were like his; no one else so laboriously verified and exhausted the facts; and no other mind rose from them, at will, into so subtile an air of meditation,—meditation too daring to be called devout, by church or world, yet too pure and lofty to merit any lower name. Lycidas has died once more, and has not left his peer.

Cape Cod does not change in its traits, but only in its boundaries, and this book will stand for it, a century hence, as it now does. It is the Cape Odyssey. Near the end, moreover, there is a remarkable chapter on previous explorers, which shows, by its patient thoroughness, and by the fearless way in which the author establishes facts which had eluded Hildreth and Bancroft, that, had he chosen history for his vocation, he could have extracted its marrow as faithfully as that of his more customary themes. Yet the grand ocean-pictures which this book contains remind us that it was the domain of external Nature which was his peculiar province; and this sublime monotone of the surges seems his fitting dirge, now that—to use the fine symbol of one who was his comrade on this very excursion—his bark has "sunk to another sea."

[1865]

Lowell's opinion of Thoreau developed through the years. In the Fable for Critics *he dismissed him as an imitator of Emerson. In his review of* A Week, *he was condescending. But in 1865, in this essay, which was ostensibly a review of Thoreau's* Letters to Various Persons, *he issued probably the most damning analysis of Thoreau that has ever been published. We must accept this as Lowell's final judgment of Thoreau, for it was this essay which he chose to appear in his collected works. But in reading it, we must keep in mind Thoreau's quarrel with Lowell over the editing of his "Chesuncook" when it appeared in Lowell's* Atlantic Monthly *in 1858 and remember that Emerson said, "Lowell . . . had a good deal of self-consciousness, and never forgave . . . Thoreau for wounding it." Since Lowell was long considered the first ranking American critic, this essay had a wide influence.*

THOREAU

BY JAMES RUSSELL LOWELL

. . . Among the pistillate plants kindled to fruitage by the Emersonian pollen, Thoreau is thus far the most remarkable; and it is something eminently fitting that his posthumous works should be offered us by Emerson, for they are strawberries from his own garden. A singular mixture of varieties, indeed, there is;—alpine, some of them, with the flavor of rare mountain air; others wood, tasting of sunny roadside banks or shy openings in the forest; and not a few seedlings swollen hugely by culture, but lacking the fine natural aroma of the more modest kinds. Strange books these are of

From the *North American Review*, CI (October, 1865), 597-608. A long, digressive introductory comment has been deleted.

his, and interesting in many ways,—instructive chiefly as showing how considerable a crop may be raised on a comparatively narrow close of mind, and how much a man may make of his life if he will assiduously follow it, though perhaps never truly finding it at last.

We have just been renewing our recollection of Mr. Thoreau's writings, and have read through his six volumes in the order of their production. We shall try to give an adequate report of their impression upon us both as critic and as mere reader. He seems to us to have been a man with so high a conceit of himself that he accepted without questioning, and insisted on our accepting, his defects and weaknesses of character as virtues and powers peculiar to himself. Was he indolent, he finds none of the activities which attract or employ the rest of mankind worthy of him. Was he wanting in the qualities that make success, it is success that is contemptible, and not himself that lacks persistency and purpose. Was he poor, money was an unmixed evil. Did his life seem a selfish one, he condemns doing good as one of the weakest of superstitions. To be of use was with him the most killing bait of the wily tempter Uselessness. He had no faculty of generalization from outside of himself, or at least no experience which would supply the material of such, and he makes his own whim the law, his own range the horizon of the universe. He condemns a world, the hollowness of whose satisfactions he had never had the means of testing, and we recognize Apemantus behind the mask of Timon. He had little active imagination; of the receptive he had much. His appreciation is of the highest quality; his critical power, from want of continuity of mind, very limited and inadequate. He somewhere cites a simile from Ossian, as an example of the superiority of the old poetry to the new, though, even were the historic evidence less convincing, the sentimental melancholy of those poems should be conclusive of their modernness. He had not artistic power such as controls a great work to the serene balance of completeness, but exquisite mechanical skill in the shaping of sentences and paragraphs, or (more rarely) short bits of verse for the expression of a detached thought, sentiment, or image. His works give one the feeling of a sky full of stars,—something impressive and exhilarating certainly, something high overhead and freckled thickly with spots of isolated brightness; but whether these have any natural relation with each other, or have any concern with our mundane matters, is for the most part matter of conjecture,— astrology as yet, and not astronomy.

It is curious, considering what Thoreau afterwards became, that he was not by nature an observer. He only saw the things he looked for, and was less poet than naturalist. Till he built his Walden shanty, he did not know that the hickory grew in Concord. Till he went to Maine, he had never seen phosphorescent wood, a phenomenon early familiar to most country boys. At forty he speaks of the seeding of the pine as a new discovery, though one should have thought that its gold-dust of blowing pollen might have earlier drawn his eye. Neither his attention nor his genius was of the spontaneous kind. He discovered nothing. He thought everything a discovery of his own, from moonlight to the planting of acorns and nuts by squirrels. This is a defect in his character, but one of his chief charms as a writer. Everything grows fresh under his hand. He delved in his mind and nature; he planted them with all manner of native and foreign seeds, and reaped assiduously. He was not merely solitary, he would be isolated, and succeeded at last in almost persuading himself that he was autochthonous. He valued everything in proportion as he fancied it to be exclusively his own. He complains in "Walden," that there is no one in Concord with whom he could talk of Oriental literature, though the man was living within two miles of his hut who had introduced him to it. This intellectual selfishness becomes sometimes almost painful in reading him. He lacked that generosity of "communication" which Johnson admired in Burke. De Quincey tells us that Wordsworth was impatient when any one else spoke of mountains, as if he had a peculiar property in them. And we can readily understand why it should be so: no one is satisfied with another's appreciation of his mistress. But Thoreau seems to have prized a lofty way of thinking (often we should be inclined to call it a remote one) not so much because it was good in itself as because he wished few to share it with him. It seems now and then as if he did not seek to lure others up "above our lower region of turmoil," but to leave his own name cut on the mountain peak as the first climber. This itch of originality infects his thought and style. To be misty is not to be mystic. He turns commonplaces end for end, and fancies it makes something new of them. As we walk down Park Street, our eye is caught by Dr. Windship's dumb-bells, one of which bears an inscription testifying that it is the heaviest ever put up at arm's length by any athlete; and in reading Mr. Thoreau's books we cannot help feeling as if he sometimes invited our attention to a particular sophism or paradox as the biggest yet maintained by any single writer. He seeks, at all risks, for perversity of thought, and revives the age of *concetti* while he fancies himself going back to a pre-classical nature. "A day," he says, "passed in the society of those Greek sages, such as described in the Banquet of Xenophon, would not be comparable with the dry wit of decayed cranberry-vines and the fresh Attic salt of the moss-beds." It is not so much the True that he loves as the Out-of-the-Way. As the Brazen Age shows itself in other men by exaggeration of phrase, so in him by extravagance of statement. He wishes always to trump your suit and to *ruff* when you least expect it. Do you love Nature because she is beautiful? He will find a better argument in her ugliness. Are you tired of the artificial man? He instantly dresses you up an ideal in a Penobscot Indian, and attributes to this creature of his otherwise-mindedness as peculiarities things that are common to all woodsmen, white or red, and this simply because he has not studied the pale-faced variety.

This notion of an absolute originality, as if one could have a patent-right in it, is an absurdity. A man cannot escape in thought, any more than he can in language, from the past and the present. As no one ever invents a word, and yet language somehow grows by general contribution and necessity, so it is with thought. Mr. Thoreau seems to us to insist in public on going back to flint and steel, when there is a match-box in his pocket which he knows very well how to use at a pinch. Originality consists in power of digesting and assimilating thought, so that they become part of our life and substance. Montaigne, for example, is one of the most original of authors, though he helped himself to ideas in every direction. But they turn to blood and coloring in his style, and give a freshness of complexion that is forever charming. In Thoreau much seems yet to be foreign and unassimilated, showing itself in symptoms of indigestion. A preacher up of Nature, we now and then detect under the surly and stoic garb something of the sophist and the sentimentalizer. We are far from implying that this was conscious on his part. But it is much easier for a man to impose on himself when he measures only with himself. A greater familiarity with ordinary men would have done Thoreau good, by showing him how many fine qualities are common to the race. The radical vice of his theory of life was, that he confounded physical with spiritual remoteness from men. One is far enough withdrawn from his fellows if he keeps himself clear of their weaknesses. He is not so truly withdrawn as exiled, if he refuse to share in their strength. It is a morbid self-consciousness that pronounces the world of men empty and worthless before trying it, the instinctive evasion of one who is sensible of some innate weakness, and retorts the accusation of it before any has made it but himself. To a healthy mind, the world is a constant challenge of opportunity. Mr. Thoreau had not a healthy mind, or he would not have been so fond of prescribing. His whole life was a search for the doctor. The old mystics had a wiser sense of what the world was worth. They ordained a severe apprenticeship to law and even ceremonial, in order to the gaining of freedom and mastery over these. Seven years of service for Rachel were to be rewarded at last with Leah. Seven other years of faithfulness with her were to win them at last the true bride of their souls. Active Life was with them the only path to the Contemplative.

Thoreau had no humor, and this implies that he was a sorry logician. Himself an artist in rhetoric, he confounds thought with style when he undertakes to speak of the latter. He was forever talking of getting away from the world, but he must be always near enough to it, nay, to the Concord corner of it, to feel the impression he makes there. He verifies the shrewd remark of Sainte-Beuve, "On touche encore à son temps et très-fort, même quand on le repousse." This egotism of his is a Stylites pillar after all, a seclusion which keeps him in the public eye. The dignity of man is an excellent thing, but therefore to hold one's self too sacred and precious is the reverse of excellent. There is something delightfully absurd in six volumes addressed to a world of such "vulgar fellows" as Thoreau affirmed his fellow-men to be. We once had a glimpse of a genuine solitary who spent his winters one hundred and fifty miles beyond all human communication, and there dwelt with his rifle as his only confidant. Compared with this, the shanty on Walden Pond has something the air, it must be confessed, of the Hermitage of La Chevrette. We do not believe that the way to a true cosmopolitanism carries one into the woods or the society of musquashes. Perhaps the narrowest provincialism is that of Self; that of Kleinwinkel is nothing to it. The natural man, like the singing birds, comes out of the forest as inevitably as the natural bear and the wildcat stick there. To seek to be natural implies a consciousness that forbids all naturalness forever. It is as easy— and no easier—to be natural in a *salon* as in a swamp, if one do not aim at it, for what we call unnaturalness always has its spring in a man's thinking too much about himself. "It is impossible," said Turgot, "for a vulgar man to be simple."

We look upon a great deal of the modern sentimentalism about Nature as a mark of disease. It is one more symptom of the general liver-complaint. In a man of wholesome constitution the wilderness is well enough for a mood or a vacation, but not for a habit of life. Those who have most loudly advertised their passion for seclusion and their intimacy with nature, from Petrarch down, have been mostly sentimentalists, unreal men, misanthropes on the spindle side, solacing an uneasy suspicion of themselves by professing contempt for their kind. They make demands on the world in advance proportioned to their inward measure of their own merit, and are angry that the world pays only by the visible measure of performance. It is true of Rousseau, the modern founder of the sect, true of St. Pierre, his intellectual child, and of Chateaubriand, his grandchild, the inventor of what we may call the primitive forest cure, and who first was touched by the solemn falling of a tree from natural decay in the windless silence of the woods. It is a very shallow view that affirms trees and rocks to be healthy, and cannot see that men in communities are just as true to the laws of their organization and destiny; that can tolerate the puffin and the fox, but not the fool and the knave; that would shun politics because of its demagogues, and snuff up the stench of the obscene fungus. The divine life of Nature is more wonderful, more various, more sublime in man than in any other of her works, and the wisdom that is gained by commerce with men, as Montaigne and Shakespeare gained it, or with one's own soul among men, as Dante, is the most delightful, as it is the most precious, of all. In outward nature it is still man that interests us, and we care far less for the things seen than the way in which poetic eyes like Wordsworth's or Thoreau's see them, and the reflections they cast there. To hear the to-do that is often made over the simple fact that a man sees the image of himself in the outward world, one is reminded of a savage when he for the first time catches a glimpse of himself in a looking-glass. "Venerable child of Nature," we are tempted to say, "to whose science in the invention of the tobacco-pipe, to whose art in the tattooing of thine undegenerate hide not yet enslaved by tailors, we are slowly striving to climb back, the miracle thou beholdest is sold in my unhappy country for a shilling!" If matters go on as they have done, and everybody must needs blab of all the favors that have been done him by roadside and river-brink and woodland walk, as if to kiss and tell were no longer treachery, it will be a positive refreshment to meet a man who is as superbly indifferent to Nature as she is to him. By and by we shall have John Smith, of No. -12, -12th Street, advertising that he is not the J. S. who saw a cowlily on Thursday last, as he never saw one in his life, would not see one if he could, and is prepared to prove an alibi on the day in question.

Solitary communion with Nature does not seem to have been sanitary or sweetening in its influence on Thoreau's character. On the contrary, his letters show him more cynical as he grew older. While he studied with respectful attention the minks and woodchucks, his neighbors, he looked with utter contempt on the august

drama of destiny of which his country was the scene, and on which
the curtain had already risen. He was converting us back to a state
of nature "so eloquently," as Voltaire said of Rousseau, "that he
almost persuaded us to go on all fours," while the wiser fates were
making it possible for us to walk erect for the first time. Had he
conversed more with his fellows, his sympathies would have
widened with the assurance that his peculiar genius had more
appreciation, and his writings a larger circle of readers, or at least
a warmer one, than he dreamed of. We have the highest testimony
to the natural sweetness, sincerity, and nobleness of his temper
and in his books an equally irrefragable one to the rare quality of
his mind. He was not a strong thinker, but a sensitive feeler. Yet
his mind strikes us as cold and wintry in its purity. A light snow
has fallen everywhere where he seems to come on the track of
the shier sensations that would elsewhere leave no trace. We think
greater compression would have done more for his fame. A feeling
of sameness comes over us as we read so much. Trifles are recorded
with an overminute punctuality and conscientiousness of detail.
We cannot help thinking sometimes of the man who

> "watches, starves, freezes, and sweats
> To learn but catechisms and alphabets
> Of unconcerning things, matters of fact,"

and sometimes of the saying of the Persian poet, that "when the
owl would boast, he boasts of catching mice at the edge of a hole."
We could readily part with some of his affectations. It was well
enough for Pythagoras to say, once for all, "When I was Euphor-
bus at the siege of Troy"; not so well for Thoreau to travesty it
into "When I was a shepherd on the plains of Assyria." A naive
thing said over again is anything but naive. But with every exception, there is no writing comparable with Thoreau's in kind, that
is comparable with it in degree where it is best; where it disengages
itself, that is, from the tangled roots and dead leaves of a secondhand Orientalism, and runs limpid and smooth and broadening as
it runs, a mirror for whatever is grand and lovely in both worlds.
George Sand says neatly, that "Art is not a study of positive

reality," *(actuality* were the fitter word,) "but a seeking after ideal truth." It would be doing very inadequate justice to Thoreau if we left it to be inferred that this ideal element did not exist in him, and that too in larger proportion, if less obtrusive, than his nature-worship. He took nature as the mountain-path to an ideal world. If the path wind a good deal, if he record too faithfully every trip over a root, if he botanize somewhat wearisomely, he gives us now and then superb outlooks from some jutting crag, and brings us out at last into an illimitable ether, where the breathing is not difficult for those who have any true touch of the climbing spirit. His shanty-life was a mere impossibility, so far as his own conception of it goes, as an entire independency of mankind. The tub of Diogenes had a sounder bottom. Thoreau's experiment actually presupposed all that complicated civilization which it theoretically abjured. He squatted on another man's land; he borrows an axe; his boards, his nails, his bricks, his mortar, his books, his lamp, his fish-hooks, his plough, his hoe, all turn state's evidence against him as an accomplice in the sin of that artificial civilization which rendered it possible that such a person as Henry D. Thoreau should exist at all. *Magnis tamen excidit ausis.* His aim was a noble and a useful one, in the direction of "plain living and high thinking." It was a practical sermon on Emerson's text that "things are in the saddle and ride mankind," an attempt to solve Carlyle's problem of "lessening your denominator." His whole life was a rebuke of the waste and aimlessness of our American luxury, which is an abject enslavement to tawdry upholstery. He had "fine trans-lunary things" in him. His better style as a writer is in keeping with the simplicity and purity of his life. We have said that his range was narrow, but to be a master is to be a master. He had caught his English at its living source, among the poets and prose-writers of its best days; his literature was extensive and recondite; his quotations are always nuggets of the purest ore; there are sentences of his as perfect as anything in the language, and thoughts as clearly crystallized; his metaphors and images are always fresh from the soil; he had watched Nature like a detective who is to go upon the stand; as we read him, it seems as if all-out-of-doors had kept a diary and become its own Montaigne; we look at the landscape as in a Claude Lorraine glass; compared with his, all other books of similar aim, even White's Selborne, seem dry as a country clergyman's meteorological journal in an old almanac.

He belongs with Donne and Browne and Novalis; if not with the originally creative men, with the scarcely smaller class who are peculiar, and whose leaves shed their invisible thought-seed like ferns.

[1872]

It was left to that "tedious archangel" Alcott, the father of the more famous Louisa May, and the most vapid and ethereal of Thoreau's Transcendentalist friends, to come down to earth and portray Thoreau's warmth. While some of Alcott's pronouncements are as "orphic" as anything he ever wrote, he at least helped to break the Stoic mold.

THOREAU

BY A. BRONSON ALCOTT

My friend and neighbor united these qualities of sylvan and human in a more remarkable manner than any whom it has been my happiness to know. Lover of the wild, he lived a borderer on the confines of civilization, jealous of the least encroachment upon his possessions.

> "Society were all but rude
> In his umbrageous solitude."

I had never thought of knowing a man so thoroughly of the country, and so purely a son of nature. I think he had the profoundest passion for it of any one of his time; and had the human sentiment been as tender and pervading, would have given us pastorals of which Virgil and Theocritus might have envied him the authorship had they chanced to be his contemporaries. As it was, he came nearer the antique spirit than any of our native poets, and touched the fields and groves and streams of his native town with

From *Concord Days* (Boston: Roberts Brothers, 1872), pp. 11-17. A digression on the origin of the Thoreau family name is deleted.

54

a classic interest that shall not fade. Some of his verses are suffused with an elegiac tenderness, as if the woods and brooks bewailed the absence of their Lycidas, and murmured their griefs meanwhile to one another,—responsive like idyls. Living in close companionship with nature, his muse breathed the spirit and voice of poetry. For when the heart is once divorced from the senses and all sympathy with common things, then poetry has fled and the love that sings.

The most welcome of companions was this plain countryman. One seldom meets with thoughts like his, coming so scented of mountain and field breezes and rippling springs, so like a luxuriant clod from under forest leaves, moist and mossy with earth-spirits. His presence was tonic, like ice-water in dog-days to the parched citizen pent in chambers and under brazen ceilings. Welcome as the gurgle of brooks and dipping of pitchers,—then drink and be cool! He seemed one with things, of nature's essence and core, knit of strong timbers,—like a wood and its inhabitants. There was in him sod and shade, wilds and waters manifold,—the mould and mist of earth and sky. Self-poised and sagacious as any denizen of the elements, he had the key to every animal's brain, every plant; and were an Indian to flower forth and reveal the scents hidden in his cranium, it would not be more surprising than the speech of our Sylvanus. He belonged to the Homeric age,—was older than pastures and gardens, as if he were of the race of heroes and one with the elements. He of all men seemed to be the native New-Englander, as much so as the oak, the granite ledge; our best sample of an indigenous American, untouched by the old country, unless he came down rather from Thor, the Northman, whose name he bore.

A peripatetic philosopher, and out-of-doors for the best part of his days and nights, he had manifold weather and seasons in him; the manners of an animal of probity and virtue unstained. Of all our moralists, he seemed the wholesomest, the busiest, and the best republican citizen in the world; always at home minding his own affairs. A little over-confident by genius, and stiffly individual, dropping clean out of his theories, while standing friendly in his strict sense of friendship, there was in him an integrity and love of justice that made possible and actual the virtues of Sparta and the Stoics,—all the more welcome in his time of shuffling and pusillanimity. Plutarch would have made him immortal in his pages had he lived before his day. Nor have we any so modern withal, so entirely his own and ours: too purely so to be appreciated at once. A scholar by birthright, and an author, his fame had not, at his decease, travelled far from the banks of the rivers he described in his books; but one hazards only the truth in affirming of his prose, that in substance and pith, it surpasses that of any naturalist of his time; and he is sure of large reading in the future. There are fairer fishes in his pages than any swimming in our streams; some sleep of his on the banks of the Merrimack by moonlight that Egypt never rivalled; a morning of which Memnon might have envied the music, and a greyhound he once had, meant for Adonis; frogs, better than any of Aristophanes; apples wilder than Adam's. His senses seemed double, giving him access to secrets not easily read by others; in sagacity resembling that of the beaver, the bee, the dog, the deer; an instinct for seeing and judging, as by some other, or seventh sense; dealing with objects as if they were shooting forth from his mind mythologically, thus completing the world all round to his senses; a creation of his at the moment. I am sure he knew the animals one by one, as most else knowable in his town; the plants, the geography, as Adam did in his Paradise, if indeed, he were not that ancestor himself. His works are pieces of exquisite sense, celebrations of Nature's virginity exemplified by rare learning, delicate art, replete with observations as accurate as original; contributions of the unique to the natural history of his country, and without which it were incomplete. Seldom has a head circumscribed so much of the sense and core of Cosmos as this footed intelligence.

If one would learn the wealth of wit there was in this plain man, the information, the poetry, the piety, he should have accompanied him on an afternoon walk to Walden, or elsewhere about the skirts of his village residence. Pagan as he might outwardly appear, yet he was the hearty worshipper of whatsoever is sound

and wholesome in nature,—a piece of russet probity and strong
sense, that nature delighted to own and honor. His talk was sug-
gestive, subtle, sincere, under as many masks and mimicries as
the shows he might pass; as significant, substantial,—nature choosing to speak through his mouth-piece,—cynically, perhaps, and
searching into the marrows of men and times he spoke of, to his
discomfort mostly and avoidance.

Nature, poetry, life,—not politics, not strict science, not society
as it is,—were his preferred themes. The world was holy, the things
seen symbolizing the things unseen, and thus worthy of worship,
calling men out-of-doors and under the firmament for health and
wholesomeness to be insinuated into their souls, not as idolators,
but as idealists. His religion was of the most primitive type, inclus-
ive of all natural creatures and things, even to "the sparrow that
falls to the ground," though never by shot of his, and for whatsoever was manly in men, his worship was comparable to that of
the priests and heroes of all time. I should say he inspired the
sentiment of love, if, indeed, the sentiment did not seem to par-
take of something purer, were that possible, but nameless from
its excellency. Certainly he was better poised and more nearly self-
reliant than other men.

> "The happy man who lived content
> With his own town, his continent,
> Whose chiding streams its banks did curb
> As ocean circumscribes its orb,
> Round which, when he his walk did take,
> Thought he performed far more than Drake;
> For other lands he took less thought
> Than this his muse and mother brought."

More primitive and Homeric than any American, his style of
thinking was robust, racy, as if Nature herself had built his sentences and seasoned the sense of his paragraphs with her own
vigor and salubrity. Nothing can be spared from them; there is
nothing superfluous; all is compact, concrete, as nature is.

His politics were of a piece with his individualism. We must
admit that he found little in political or religious establishments

answering to his wants, that his attitude was defiant, if not annihilating, as if he had said to himself:—

"The state is man's pantry at most, and filled at an enormous cost,—a spoliation of the human common-wealth. Let it go. Heroes can live on nuts, and free-men sun themselves in the clefts of rocks, rather than sell their liberty for this pottage of slavery. We, the few honest neighbors, can help one another; and should the state ask any favors of us, we can take the matter into consideration leisurely, and at our convenience give a respectful answer.

"But why require a state to protect one's rights? the man is all. Let him husband himself; needs he other servant or runner? Self-keeping is the best economy. That is a great age when the state is nothing and man is all. He founds himself in freedom, and maintains his uprightness therein; founds an empire and maintains states. Just retire from those concerns, and see how soon they must needs go to pieces, the sooner for the virtue thus withdrawn from them. All the manliness of individuals is sunk in that partnership in trade. Not only must I come out of institutions but come out of myself, if I will be free and independent. Shall one be denied the privilege on coming of mature age of choosing whether he will be a citizen of the country he happens to be born in, or another? And what better title to a spot of ground than being a man, and having none? Is not man superior to state or country? I plead exemption from all interference by men or states with my individual prerogatives. That is mine which none can steal from me, nor is that yours which I or any man can take away."

> "I am too high born to be propertied,
> To be a secondary at control,
> Or useful serving man and instrument
> To any sovereign state throughout the world." . . .

[1880]

Along with the Emerson and Lowell essays, Stevenson's was one of the three most influential in shaping public opinion of Thoreau. It crystallized in the people's mind the picture of Thoreau as a skulker.

HENRY DAVID THOREAU: HIS CHARACTER AND OPINIONS

BY ROBERT LOUIS STEVENSON

I

Thoreau's thin, penetrating, big-nosed face, even in a bad wood-cut, conveys some hint of the limitations of his mind and character. With his almost acid sharpness of insight, with his almost animal dexterity in act, there went none of that large, unconscious geniality of the world's heroes. He was not easy, not ample, not urbane, not even kind; his enjoyment was hardly smiling, or the smile was not broad enough to be convincing; he had no waste lands nor kitchen-midden in his nature, but was all improved and sharpened to a point. "He was bred to no profession," says Emerson; "he never married, he lived alone; he never went to church; he never voted; he refused to pay a tax to the state; he ate no flesh, he drank no wine, he never knew the use of tobacco; and, though a naturalist, he used neither trap nor gun. When asked at dinner what dish he preferred, he answered, 'The nearest.'" So many negative superiorities begin to smack a little of the prig. From his

From *Cornhill Magazine*, XLI (June, 1880), 665-82.

later works he was in the habit of cutting out humorous passages, under the impression that they were beneath the dignity of his moral muse; and there we see the prig stand public and confessed. It was "much easier," says Emerson, acutely, much easier for Thoreau to say *no* than *yes;* and that is a characteristic which depicts the man. It is a useful accompaniment to be able to say *no,* but surely it is the essence of amiability to prefer to say *yes* where it is possible. There is something wanting in the man who does not hate himself whenever he is constrained to say no. And there was a great deal wanting in this born dissenter. He was almost shockingly devoid of weaknesses; he had not enough of them to be truly polar with humanity; whether you call him demi-god or demi-man, he was at least not altogether one of us, for he was not touched with a feeling of our infirmities. The world's heroes have room for all positive qualities, even those which are disreputable, in the capacious theatre of their dispositions. Such can live many lives; while a Thoreau can live but one, and that only with perpetual foresight.

He was no ascetic, rather an Epicurean of the nobler sort; and he had this one great merit, that he succeeded so far as to be happy. "I love my fate to the core and rind," he wrote once; and even while he lay dying, here is what he dictated (for it seems he was already too feeble to control the pen): "You ask particularly after my health. I *suppose* that I have not many months to live, but of course know nothing about it. I may say that I am enjoying existence as much as ever, and regret nothing." It is not given to all to bear so clear a testimony to the sweetness of their fate, nor to any without courage and wisdom; for this world in itself is but a painful and uneasy place of residence, and lasting happiness, at least to the self-conscious, comes only from within. Now, Thoreau's content and ectasy in living was, we may say, like a plant that he had watered and tended with womanish solicitude; for there is apt to be something unmanly, something almost dastardly, in a life that does not move with dash and freedom, and that fears the bracing contact of the world. In one word, Thoreau was a skulker. He did not wish virtue to go out of him among his fellow-men, but slunk into a corner to hoard it for himself. He left all for the sake of certain virtuous self-indulgences. It is true that his tastes were noble; that his ruling passion was to keep himself unspotted from the world; and that his luxuries were all of the same healthy order as cold tubs and early rising. But a man may be both coldly cruel in the pursuit of goodness, and morbid even in the pursuit of health. I cannot lay my hands on the passage in which he explains his abstinence from tea and coffee, but I am sure I have the meaning correctly. It is this: He thought it bad economy and worthy of no true virtuoso to spoil the natural rapture of the morning with such muddy stimulants; let him but see the sun rise, and he was already sufficiently inspirited for the labors of the day. That may be reason good enough to abstain from tea; but when we go on to find the same man, on the same or similar grounds, abstain from nearly everything that his neighbors innocently and pleasurably use, and from the rubs and trials of human society itself into the bargain, we recognize that valetudinarian healthfulness which is more delicate than sickness itself. We need have no respect for a state of artificial training. True health is to be able to do without it. Shakespeare, we can imagine, might begin the day upon a quart of ale, and yet enjoy the sunrise to the full as much as Thoreau, and commemorate his enjoyment in vastly better verses. A man who must separate himself from his neighbors' habits in order to be happy, is in much the same case with one who requires to take opium for the same purpose. What we want to see is one who can breast into the world, do a man's work, and still preserve his first and pure enjoyment of existence.

Thoreau's faculties were of a piece with his moral shyness; for they were all delicacies. He could guide himself about the woods on the darkest night by the touch of his feet. He could pick up an exact dozen of pencils by the feeling, pace distances with accuracy, and gauge cubic contents by the eye. His smell was so dainty that he could perceive the fetor of dwelling-houses as he passed them by at night; his palate so unsophisticated that, like a child, he disliked the taste of wine—or perhaps, living in America, had never tasted any that was good; and his knowledge of nature was so complete and curious that he could have told the time of year, within a day or so, by the aspect of the plants. In his dealings with animals, he was the original of Hawthorne's Donatello. He pulled the woodchuck out of its hole by the tail; the hunted fox came to him for protection; wild squirrels have been seen to nestle in his waistcoat; he would thrust his arm into a pool and bring forth a bright, panting fish, lying undismayed in the palm of his hand. There were few things that he could not do. He could make a house, a boat, a pencil, or a book. He was a surveyor, a scholar, a natural historian. He could run, walk, climb, skate, swim and manage a boat. The smallest occasion served to display his physical accomplishment; and a manufacturer from merely observing his dexterity with the window of a railway carriage, offered him a situation on the spot. "The only fruit of much living," he observes, "is the ability to do some slight thing better." But such was the exactitude of his senses, so alive was he in every fibre, that it seems as if the maxim should be changed in his case, for he could do most things with unusual perfection. And perhaps he had an approving eye to himself when he wrote: "Though the youth at last grows indifferent, the laws of the universe are not indifferent, *but are forever on the side of the most sensitive.*"

II

Thoreau had decided, it would seem, from the very first to lead a life of self-improvement: the needle did not tremble as with richer natures, but pointed steadily north; and as he saw duty and inclination in one, he turned all his strength in that direction. He was met upon the threshold by a common difficulty. In this world, in spite of its many agreeable features, even the most sensitive must undergo some drudgery to live. It is not possible to devote your time to study and meditation without what are quaintly but happily denominated private means; these absent, a man must contrive to earn his bread by some service to the public such as the public cares to pay him for; or, as Thoreau loved to put it, Apollo must serve Admetus. This was to Thoreau even a sourer necessity than it is to most; there was a love of freedom, a strain of the wild man, in his nature, that rebelled with violence against the yoke of custom; and he was so eager to cultivate himself and to be happy in his own society, that he could consent with difficulty even to the interruptions of friendship. *"Such are my engagements to myself* that I dare not promise," he once wrote in answer to an invitation; and the italics are his own. Marcus Aurelius found time to study virtue, and between whiles to conduct the imperial affairs of Rome; but Thoreau is so busy improving himself, that he must think twice about a morning call. And now imagine him condemned for eight hours a day to some uncongenial and unmeaning business! He shrank from the very look of the mechanical in life; all should if possible, be sweetly spontaneous and swimmingly progressive. Thus he learned to make lead-pencils, and, when he had gained the best certificate and his friends began to congratulate him on his establishment in life, calmly announced that he should never make another. "Why should I?" he said; "I would not do again what I have done once." For when a thing has once been done as well as it wants to be, it is of no further interest to the self-improver. Yet in after years, and when it became needful to support his family, he returned patiently to this mechanical art—a step more than worthy of himself.

The pencils seem to have been Apollo's first experiment in the service of Admetus; but others followed. "I have thoroughly tried school-keeping," he writes, "and found that my expenses were in proportion, or rather out of proportion, to my income; for I was obliged to dress and train, not to say think and believe, accordingly, and I lost my time into the bargain. As I did not teach for the benefit of my fellow-men, but simply for a livelihood, this was a failure. I have tried trade; but I found that it would take ten years to get under way in that, and that then I should probably be on my way to the devil." Nothing, indeed, can surpass his scorn for all so-called business. Upon that subject, gall squirts from him at a touch. "The whole enterprise of this nation is not illustrated by a thought," he writes; "it is not warmed by a sentiment; there is nothing in it for which a man should lay down his life, nor even his gloves."

And again: "If our merchants did not most of them fail, and the banks too, my faith in the old laws of this world would be staggered. The statement that ninety-six in a hundred doing such business surely break down is perhaps the sweetest fact that statistics have revealed." The wish was probably father to the figures; but there is something enlivening in a hatred of so genuine a brand, hot as Corsican revenge and sneering like Voltaire.

Pencils, school-keeping, and trade being thus discarded one after another, Thoreau, with a stroke of strategy, turned the position. He saw his way to get his board and lodging for practically nothing; and Admetus never got less work out of any servant since the world began. It was his ambition to be an Oriental philosopher; but he was always a very Yankee sort of Oriental. Even in the peculiar attitude in which he stood to money, his system of personal economics, as we may call it, he displayed a vast amount of truly down-east calculation, and he adopted poverty like a piece of business. Yet his system is based on one or two ideas which, I believe, come naturally to all thoughtful youths, and are only pounded out of them by city uncles. Indeed, something essentially youthful distinguishes all Thoreau's knock-down blows at current opinion. Like the posers of a child, they leave the orthodox in a kind of speechless agony. These know the thing is nonsense. They are sure there must be an answer, yet somehow cannot find it. So it is with his system of economy. He cuts through the subject on so new a plane that the accepted arguments apply no longer; he attacks it in a new dialect where there are no catchwords ready made for the defender; after you have been boxing for years on a polite, gladiatorial convention, here is an assailant who does not scruple to hit below the belt.

"The cost of a thing," says he, "is *the amount of what I will call life* which is required to be exchanged for it, immediately or in the long run." I have been accustomed to put it to myself, perhaps more clearly, that the price we have to pay for money is paid in liberty. Between these two ways of it, at least, the reader will probably not fail to find a third definition of his own; and it follows, on one or other, that a man may pay too dearly for his livelihood, by giving, in Thoreau's terms, his whole life for it, or, in mine, bartering for it the whole of his available liberty, and becoming a slave till death. There are two questions to be considered— the quality of what we buy, and the price we have to pay for it. Do you want a thousand a year, a two thousand a year, or a ten thousand a year livelihood? and can you afford the one you want? It is a matter of taste; it is not in the least degree a question of duty, though commonly supposed so. But there is no authority for that view anywhere. It is nowhere in the Bible. It is true that we might do a vast amount of good if we were wealthy, but it is also highly improbable; not many do; and the art of growing rich is not only quite distinct from that of doing good, but the practice of the one does not at all train a man for practising the other. "Money might be of great service to me," writes Thoreau; "but the difficulty now is that I do not improve my opportunities, and therefore I am not prepared to have my opportunities increased." It is a mere illusion that, above a certain income, the personal desires will be satisfied and leave a wider margin for the generous impulse. It is as difficult to be generous, or anything else, except perhaps a member of Parliament, on thirty thousand as on two hundred a year.

Now Thoreau's tastes were well defined. He loved to be free, to be master of his time and seasons, to indulge the mind rather than the body; he preferred long rambles to rich dinners, his own reflections to the consideration of society, and an easy, calm, unfettered, active life among green trees to dull toiling at the counter of a bank. And such being his inclination he determined to gratify it. A poor man must save off something; he determined to save off his livelihood. "When a man has attained those things which are necessary to life," he writes, "there is another alternative than to obtain the superfluities; *he may adventure on life now, his vacation from humbler toil having commenced.*" Thoreau would get shelter, some kind of covering for his body, and necessary daily bread; even these he should get as cheaply as possible; and then, his vacation from humbler toil having commenced, devote himself to Oriental philosophers, the study of nature, and the work of self-improvement.

Prudence, which bids us all go to the ant for wisdom and hoard against the day of sickness, was not a favorite with Thoreau. He preferred that other, whose name is so much misappropriated, Faith. When he had secured the necessaries of the moment, he would not reckon up possible accidents or torment himself with trouble for the future. He had no toleration for the man "who ventures to live only by the aid of the mutual insurance company, which has promised to bury him decently." He would trust himself a little to the world. "We may safely trust a good deal more than we do," says he. "How much is not done by us! or what if we had been taken sick?" And then, with a stab of satire, he describes contemporary mankind in a phrase: "All the day long on the alert, at night we unwillingly say our prayers and commit ourselves to uncertainties." It is not likely that the public will be much affected by Thoreau, when they blink the direct injunctions of the religion they profess; and yet, whether we will or no, we make the same hazardous ventures; we back our own health and the honesty of our neighbors for all that we are worth; and it is chilling to think how many must lose their wager.

In 1845, twenty-eight years old, an age by which the liveliest have usually declined into some conformity with the world, Thoreau, with a capital of something less than five pounds and a borrowed axe, walked forth into the woods by Walden Pond, and began his new experiment in life. He built himself a dwelling, and returned the axe, he says with characteristic and workmanlike pride, sharper than when he borrowed it; he reclaimed a patch, where he cultivated beans, peas, potatoes, and sweet corn; he had his bread to bake, his farm to dig, and for the matter of six weeks in the summer he worked at surveying, carpentry, or some other of his numerous dexterities, for hire. For more than five years, this was all that he required for his support, and he had the winter and most of the summer at his entire disposal. For six weeks of occupation, a little cooking and a little hygienic gardening, the man, you may say, had as good as stolen his livelihood.

Or we must rather allow that he had done far better; for the thief himself is continually and busily occupied; and even one born to inherit a million will have more calls upon his time than Thoreau. Well might he say, "What old people tell you you cannot do, you try and find you can." And how surprising is his conclusion: "I am convinced that *to maintain one's self on this earth is not a hardship, but a pastime, if we will live simply and wisely; as the pursuits of simpler nations are still the sports of the more artificial.*"

When he had enough of that kind of life, he showed the same simplicity in giving it up as in beginning it. There are some who could have done the one, but, vanity forbidding, not the other; and that is perhaps the story of the hermits; but Thoreau made no fetich of his own example, and did what he wanted squarely. And five years is long enough for an experiment and to prove the success of transcendental Yankeeism. It is not his frugality which is worthy of note; for, to begin with, that was inborn, and therefore inimitable by others who are differently constituted; and again, it was no new thing, but has often been equalled by poor Scotch students at the universities. The point is the sanity of his view of life, and the insight with which he recognized the position of money, and thought out for himself the problem of riches and a livelihood. Apart from his eccentricities, he had perceived, and was acting on, a truth of universal application. For money enters in two different characters into the scheme of life. A certain amount, varying with the number and empire of our desires, is a true necessary to each one of us in the present order of society; but beyond that amount, money is a commodity to be bought or not to be bought, a luxury in which we may either indulge or stint ourselves, like any other. And there are many luxuries that we may legitimately prefer to it, such as a grateful conscience, a country life, or the woman of our inclination. Trite, flat, and obvious as this conclusion may appear, we have only to look round us in society to see how scantily it has been recognized; and perhaps even ourselves, after a little reflection, may decide to spend a trifle less for money, and indulge ourselves a trifle more in the article of freedom.

III

"To have done anything by which you earned money merely," says Thoreau, "is to be" (have been, he means,) "idle and worse." There are two passages in his letters, both oddly enough, relating to firewood, which must be brought together to be rightly understood. So taken, they contain between them the marrow of all good sense on the subject of work in its relation to something broader than mere livelihood. Here is the first: "I suppose I have burned up a good-sized tree to-night—and for what? I settled with Mr. Tarbell for it the other day; but that wasn't the final settlement. I got off cheaply from him. At last one will say: 'Let us see, how much wood did you burn, sir?' And I shall shudder to think that the next question will be, 'What did you do while you were warm?'" Even after we have settled with Admetus in the person of Mr. Tarbell, there comes, you see, a further question. It is not enough to have earned our livelihood. Either the earning itself should have been serviceable to mankind, or something else must follow. To live is sometimes very difficult, but it is never meritorious in itself; and we must have a reason to allege to our own conscience why we should continue to exist upon this crowded earth. If Thoreau had simply dwelt in his house at Walden, a lover of trees, birds, and fishes, and the open air and virtue, a reader of wise books, an idle, selfish self-improver, he would have managed to cheat Admetus, but, to cling to metaphor, the devil would have had him in the end. Those who can avoid toil altogether and dwell in the Arcadia of private means, and even those who can, by abstinence, reduce the necessary amount of it to some six weeks a year, having the more liberty, have only the higher moral obligation to be up and doing in the interest of man.

The second passage is this: "There is a far more important and warming heat, commonly lost, which precedes the burning of the wood. It is the smoke of industry, which is incense. I had been so thoroughly warmed in body and spirit, that when at length my fuel was housed, I came near selling it to the ashman, as if I had extracted all its heat." Industry is, in itself and when properly chosen, delightful and profitable to the worker; and when your toil has been a pleasure, you have not, as Thoreau says, "earned money merely," but money, health, delight, and moral profit all in one. "We must heap up a great pile of doing for a small diameter of being," he says in another place; and then exclaims, "How admirably the artist is made to accomplish his self-culture by devotion to his art!" We may escape uncongenial toil, only to devote ourselves to that which is congenial. It is only to transact some higher business that even Apollo dare play the truant from Admetus. We must all work for the sake of work; we must all work, as Thoreau says again, in any "absorbing pursuit—it does not much matter what, so it be honest;" but the most profitable work is that which combines into one continued effort the largest proportion of the powers and desires of a man's nature; that into which he will plunge with ardor, and from which he will desist with reluctance; in which he will know the weariness of fatigue, but not that of satiety; and which will be ever fresh, pleasing, and stimulating to his taste. Such work holds a man together, braced at all points; it does not suffer him to doze or wander; it keeps him actively conscious of himself, yet raised among superior interests; it gives him the profit of industry with the pleasures of a pastime. This is what his art should be to the true artist, and that to a degree unknown in other and less intimate pursuits. For other professions stand apart from the human business of life; but an art has its seat at the centre of the artist's doings and sufferings, deals directly with his experiences, teaches him the lessons of his own fortunes and mishaps, and becomes a part of his biography. So, says Goethe:

> "Spät erklingt was früh erklang;
> Glück und Unglück wird Gesang."

Now Thoreau's art was literature; and it was one of which he had conceived most ambitiously. He loved and believed in good books. He said well, "Life is not habitually seen from any common platform so truly and unexaggerated as in the light of literature." But the literature he loved was of the heroic order. "Books, not which afford us a cowering enjoyment, but in which each thought is of unusual daring; such as an idle man cannot read, and a timid one would not be entertained by; which even make us dangerous to existing institutions—such I call good books." He did not think them easy to be read. "The heroic books," he says, "even if printed in the character of our mother-tongue, will always be in a language dead to degenerate times; and we must laboriously seek the meaning of each word and line, conjecturing a larger sense than common use permits out of what wisdom and valor and generosity we have." Nor does he suppose that such books are easily written. "Great prose, of equal elevation, commands our respect more than great verse," says he, "since it implies a more permanent and level height, a life more pervaded with the grandeur of the thought. The poet often only makes an irruption, like the Parthian, and is off again, shooting while he retreats; but the prose writer has conquered like a Roman and settled colonies." We may ask ourselves, almost with dismay, whether such works exist at all but in the imagination of the student. For the bulk of the best of books is apt to be made up with ballast; and those in which energy of thought is combined with any stateliness of utterance may be almost counted on the fingers. Looking round in English for a book that should answer Thoreau's two demands of a style like poetry and sense that shall be both original and inspiriting, I come to Milton's *Areopagitica,* and can name no other instance for the moment. Two things at least are plain: that if a man will condescend to nothing more commonplace in the way of reading, he must not look to have a large library, and that if he proposes himself to write in a similar vein, he will find his work cut out for him.

Thoreau composed seemingly while he walked, or at least exercise and composition were with him intimately connected; for we are told that "the length of his walk uniformly made the length of his writing." He speaks in one place of "plainness and vigor, the ornaments of style," which is rather too paradoxical to be comprehensively true. In another he remarks: "As for style of writing, if one has anything to say it drops from him simply as a stone falls to the ground." We must conjecture a very large sense indeed for the phrase "if one has anything to say." When truth flows from a man, fittingly clothed in style and without conscious effort, it is because the effort has been made and the work practically completed before he sat down to write. It is only out of fulness of thinking that expression drops perfect like a ripe fruit; and when Thoreau wrote so nonchalantly at his desk, it was because he had been vigorously active during his walk. For neither clearness, compression, nor beauty of language come to any living creature till after a busy and a prolonged acquaintance with the subject on hand. Easy writers are those who, like Walter Scott, choose to remain contented with a less degree of perfection than is legitimately within the compass of their powers. We hear of Shakespeare and his clean manuscript; but in face of the evidence of the style itself and of the various editions of "Hamlet," this merely proves that Messrs. Hemming and Condell were unacquainted with the common enough phenomenon called a fair copy. He who would recast a tragedy already given to the world must frequently and earnestly have revised details in the study. Thoreau himself, and in spite of his protestations, is an instance of even extreme research in one direction; and his effort after heroic utterance is proved not only by the occasional finish, but by the determined exaggeration of his style. "I trust you realize what an exaggerator I am—that I lay myself out to exaggerate," he writes. And again, hinting at the explanation: "Who that has heard a strain of music feared lest he should speak extravagantly any more forever?" And yet once more, in his essay on Carlyle, and this time with his meaning well in hand: "No truth, we think, was ever expressed but with this sort of emphasis, that for the time there seemed to be no other." Thus Thoreau was an exaggerative and a parabolical writer, not because he loved the literature of the East, but from a desire that people should understand and realize what he was writing. He was near the truth upon the general question; but in his own particular method, it appears to me, he wandered. Literature is not less a conventional art than painting or sculpture; and it is the least striking, as it is the most comprehensive, of the three. To hear a strain of music, to see a beautiful woman, a river, a great city, or a starry night is to make a man despair of his Lilliputian arts in language. Now, to gain that emphasis which seems denied to us by the very nature of the medium, the proper method of literature is by selection, which is a kind of negative exaggeration. It is the right of the literary artist, as Thoreau was on the point of seeing, to leave out whatever does not suit his purpose. Thus we extract the pure gold; and thus the well-written story of a noble life becomes, by its very omissions, more thrilling to the reader. But to go beyond this, like Thoreau, and to exaggerate directly, is to leave the saner classical tradition, and to put the reader on his guard. And when you write the whole for the half, you do not express your thought more forcibly, but only express a different thought which is not yours.

Thoreau's true subject was the pursuit of self-improvement combined with an unfriendly criticism of life as it goes on in our societies; it is there that he best displays the freshness and surprising trenchancy of his intellect; it is there that his style becomes plain and vigorous, and therefore, according to his own formula, ornamental. Yet he did not care to follow this vein singly, but must drop into it by the way in books of a different purport. *Walden, or Life in the Woods, A Week on the Concord and Merrimack Rivers, The Maine Woods,* such are the titles he affects. He was probably reminded by his delicate critical perception that the true business of literature is with narrative; in reasoned narrative, and there alone, that art enjoys all its advantages, and suffers least from its defects. Dry precept and disembodied disquisition, as they can only be read with an effort*of abstraction, can never convey a complete or perfectly natural impression. Truth, even in literature, must be clothed with flesh and blood, or it cannot tell its whole story to the reader. Hence the effect of anecdote on simple minds; and hence good biographies and works of high, imaginative art are not only far more entertaining, but far more edifying, than books of theory or precept. Now, Thoreau could not clothe his opinions in the garment of art, for that was not his talent; but he sought to gain the same elbow-room for himself, and to afford a similar relief to his readers, by mingling his thoughts with a record of experience.

Again, he was a lover of nature. The quality which we should call mystery in a painting, and which belongs so particularly to the aspect of the external world and to its influence upon our feelings, was one which he was never weary of attempting to reproduce in his books. The seeming significance of nature's appearances, their unchanging strangeness to the senses, and the thrilling response which they waken in the mind of man, continued to surprise and stimulate his spirits. It appeared to him, I think, that if we could only write near enough to the facts, and yet with no pedestrian calm, but ardently, we might transfer the glamour of reality direct upon our pages; and that, if it were once thus captured and expressed, a new and instructive relation might appear between men's thoughts and the phenomena of nature. This was the eagle that he pursued all his life long, like a schoolboy with a butterfly net. Hear him to a friend: "Let me suggest a theme to you—to state to yourself precisely and completely what that walk over the mountains amounted to for you, returning to this essay again and again until you are satisfied that all that was important in your experience is in it. Don't suppose that you can tell it precisely the first dozen times you try, but at 'em again; especially when, after a sufficient pause, you suspect that you are touching the heart or summit of the matter, reiterate your blows there, and account for the mountain to yourself. Not that the story need be long, but it will take a long while to make it short." Such was the method, not consistent for a man whose meanings were to "drop from him as a stone falls to the ground." Perhaps the most successful work that Thoreau ever accomplished in this direction is to be found in the passages relating to the fish in the *Week*. These are remarkable for the vivid truth of impression and a happy suitability of language, not frequently surpassed.

Whatever Thoreau tried to do was tried in fair, square prose, with sentences solidly built, and no help from bastard rhythms. Moreover, there is a progression—I cannot call it a progress—in

his work toward a more and more strictly prosaic level, until at last
he sinks into the bathos of the prosy. Emerson mentions having
once remarked to Thoreau; "Who would not like to write something which all can read, like *Robinson Crusoe?* and who does
not see with regret that his page is not solid with a right materialistic treatment which delights everybody?" I must say in passing
that it is not the right materialistic treatment which delights
the world in *Robinson,* but the romantic and philosophic interest
of the fable. The same treatment does quite the reverse of delight-
ing us when it is applied, in *Colonel Jack,* to the management of
a plantation. But I cannot help suspecting Thoreau to have been
influenced either by this identical remark or by some other closely
similar in meaning. He began to fall more and more into a detailed
materialistic treatment; he went into the business doggedly, as one
who should make a guide-book; he not only chronicled what had
been important in his own experience, but whatever might have
been important in the experience of anybody else; not only what
had affected him, but all that he saw or heard. His ardor had grown
less, or perhaps it was inconsistent with a right materialistic treatment to display such emotions as he felt; and, to complete the
eventful change, he chose, from a sense of moral dignity, to gut
these later works of the saving quality of humor. He was not one
of those authors who have learned, in his own words, "to leave
out their dulness." He inflicts his full quantity upon the reader
in such books as *Cape Cod,* or *The Yankee in Canada.* Of the
latter he confessed that he had not managed to get much of himself into it. God knows he had not, nor yet much of Canada, we
may hope. "Nothing," he says somewhere, "can shock a brave
man but dulness." Well, there are few spots more shocking to the
brave than the pages of *The Yankee in Canada.*

There are but three books of his that will be read with much
pleasure: the *Week, Walden,* and the collected letters. As to his
poetry, Emerson's word shall suffice for us, it is so accurate and
so prettily said: "The thyme and marjoram are not yet honey."
In this, as in his prose, he relied greatly on the good will of the
reader, and wrote throughout in faith. It was an exercise of faith

to suppose that many would understand the sense of his best work, or that any could be exhilarated by the dreary chronicling of his worst. "But," as he says, "the gods do not hear any rude or discordant sound, as we learn from the echo; and I know that the nature toward which I launch these sounds is so rich that it will modulate anew and wonderfully improve my rudest strain."

IV

"What means the fact," he cries, "that a soul which has lost all hope for itself can inspire in another listening soul such an infinite confidence in it, even while it is expressing its despair?" The question is an echo and an illustration of the words last quoted; and it forms the key-note of his thoughts on friendship. No one else, to my knowledge, has spoken in so high and just a spirit of the kindly relations; and I doubt if it be a drawback that these lessons should come from one in many ways so unfitted to be a teacher in this branch. The very coldness and egoism of his own intercourse gave him a clearer insight into the intellectual basis of our warm, mutual tolerations; and testimony to their worth comes with added force from one who was solitary and disobliging, and of whom a friend remarked, with equal wit and wisdom, "I love Henry, but I cannot like him."

He can hardly be persuaded to make any distinction between love and friendship; in such rarefied and freezing air, upon the mountain-tops of meditation, had he taught himself to breathe. He was, indeed, too accurate an observer not to have remarked that "there exists already a natural disinterestedness and liberality" between men and women; yet, he thought, "friendship is no respecter of sex." Perhaps there is a sense in which the words are true; but they were spoken in ignorance; and perhaps we shall have put the matter most correctly, if we call love a foundation for a nearer and freer degree of friendship than can be possible without it. For there are delicacies, eternal between persons of the same sex, which are melted and disappear in the warmth of love. To both, if they are to be right, he attributes the same nature and condition. "We are not what we are," says he, "nor do we treat or esteem each other for such, but for what we are capable of being." "A friend is one who incessantly pays us the compliment of expecting all the virtues from us and who can appreciate them in us." "The friend asks no return but that his friend will religiously accept and wear and not disgrace his apotheosis of him." "It is the merit and preservation of friendship that it takes place on a level higher than the actual characters of the parties would seem to warrant." This is to put friendship on a pedestal indeed; and yet the root of the matter is there; and the last sentence, in particular, is like a light in a dark place, and makes many mysteries plain. We are different with different friends; yet if we look closely we shall find that every such relation reposes on some particular apotheosis of one's self; with each friend, although we could not distinguish it in words from any other, we have at least one special reputation to preserve; and it is thus that we run, when mortified, to our friend or the woman that we love, not to hear ourselves called better, but to be better men in point of fact. We seek this society to flatter ourselves with our own good conduct. And hence any falsehood in the relation, any incomplete or perverted understanding, will spoil even the pleasure of these visits. Thus says Thoreau again: "Only lovers know the value of truth." And yet again: "They ask for words and deeds when a true relation is word and deed."

But it follows that since they are neither of them so good as the other hopes, and each is, in a very honest manner, playing a part above his powers, such an intercourse must often be disappointing to both. "We may bid farewell sooner than complain," says Thoreau, "for our complaint is too well grounded to be uttered." "We have not so good a right to hate any as our friend."

> "It were treason to our love
> And a sin to God above,
> One iota to abate
> Of a pure, impartial hate."

Love is not blind, nor yet forgiving. "O yes, believe me," as the song says, "Love has eyes!" The nearer the intimacy, the more cuttingly do we feel the unworthiness of those we love; and because you love one, and would die for that love to-morrow, you have not forgiven, and you never will forgive, that friend's misconduct. If you want a person's faults, go to those who love him. They will not tell you, but they know. And herein lies the magnanimous courage of love, that it endures this knowledge without change.

It required a cold, distant personality like that of Thoreau, perhaps to recognize and certainly to utter this truth; for a more human love makes it a point of honor not to acknowledge those faults of which it is most conscious. But his point of view is both high and dry. He has no illusions; he does not give way to love any more than to hatred; but preserves them both with care, like valuable curiosities. A more bald-headed picture of life, if I may so express myself, or a more selfish, has seldom been presented. He is an egotist; he does not remember, or does not think it worth while to remark, that, in these near intimacies, we are ninety-nine times disappointed in our beggarly selves for once that we are disappointed in our friend; that it is we who seem most frequently undeserving of the love that unites us; and that it is by our friend's conduct that we are continually rebuked and yet strengthened for a fresh endeavor. Thoreau is dry, priggish, and selfish. It is profit he is after in these intimacies; moral profit, certainly, but still profit to himself. If you will be the sort of friend I want, he remarks naively, "my education cannot dispense with your society." His education! as though a friend were a dictionary. And with all this, not one word about pleasure, or laughter, or kisses, or any quality of flesh and blood. It was not inappropriate, surely, that he had such close relations with the fish. We can understand the friend already quoted, when he cried: "As for taking his arm, I would as soon think of taking the arm of an elm-tree!"

As a matter of fact he experienced but a broken enjoyment in his intimacies. He says he has been perpetually on the brink of the sort of intercourse he wanted, and yet never completely attained it. And what else had he to expect when he would not, in a happy phrase of Carlyle's, "nestle down into it?" Truly, so it will be always if you only stroll in upon your friends as you might stroll in to see a cricket match; and even then not simply for the pleasure of the thing, but with some afterthought of self-improvement, as though you had come to the cricket match to bet. It was his theory that people saw each other too frequently, so that their curiosity was not properly whetted, nor had they anything fresh to communicate; but friendship must be something else than a society for mutual improvement—indeed, it must only be that by the way, and to some extent unconsciously; and if Thoreau had been a man instead of a manner of elm tree, he would have felt that he saw his friends too seldom, and have reaped benefits unknown to his philosophy from a more sustained and easy intercourse. We might remind him of his own words about love: "We should have no reserve; we should give the whole of ourselves to that business. But commonly men have not imagination enough to be thus employed about a human being, but must be coopering a barrel, forsooth." Ay, or reading Oriental philosophers. It is not the nature of the rival occupation, it is the fact that you suffer it to be a rival, that renders loving intimacy impossible. Nothing is given for nothing in this world; there can be no true love, even on your own side, without devotion; devotion is the exercise of love, by which it grows; but if you will give enough of that, if you will pay the price in a sufficient "amount of what you call life," why then indeed, whether with wife or comrade, you may have months and even years of such easy, natural, pleasurable, and yet improving intercourse as shall make time a moment and kindness a delight.

The secret of his retirement lies not in misanthropy, of which he had no tincture, but part in his engrossing design of self-improvement and part in the real deficiencies of social intercourse. He was not so much difficult about his fellow human beings as he could not tolerate the terms of their association. He could take to a man for any genuine qualities, as we see by his admirable sketch of the Canadian wood-cutter in *Walden;* but he would not consent, in his own words, to "feebly fabulate and paddle in the social slush." It seemed to him, I think, that society is precisely the reverse of friendship, in that it takes place on a lower level than the characters of any of the parties would warrant us to expect. The society talk of even the most brilliant man is of greatly less account than what you will get from him in (as the French say) a little committee. And Thoreau wanted geniality; he had not enough of the superficial, even, at command; he could not swoop into a parlor and, in the naval phrase "cut.out" a human being from that dreary port; nor had he inclination for the task. I suspect he loved books and nature as well and near as warmly as he loved his fellow-creatures: a melancholy, lean degeneration of the human character.

"As for the dispute about solitude and society," he thus sums up, "any comparison is impertinent. It is an idling down on the plain at the base of the mountain instead of climbing steadily to its top. Of course you will be glad of all the society you can get to go up with? Will you go to glory with me? is the burden of the song. It is not that we love to be alone, but that we love to soar, and when we do soar the company grows thinner and thinner till there is none at all. It is either the tribune on the plain, a sermon on the mount, or a very private ecstasy still higher up. Use all the society that will abet you." But surely it is no very extravagant opinion that it is better to give than to receive, to serve than to use our companions; and above all, where there is no question of service upon either side, that it is good to enjoy their company like a natural man. It is curious and in some ways dispiriting that a writer may be always best corrected out of his own mouth; and so, to conclude, here is another passage from Thoreau, which seems aimed directly at himself: "Do not be too moral; you may cheat yourself out of much life so. . . . *All fables, indeed, have their morals; but the innocent enjoy the story.*"

V

"The only obligation," says he, "which I have a right to assume is to do at any time what I think right." "Why should we ever go abroad, even across the way, to ask a neighbor's advice?" "There is a nearer neighbor within, who is incessantly telling us how we should behave. *But we wait for the neighbor without to tell us of some false, easier way.*" "The greater part of what my neighbors call good I believe in my soul to be bad." To be what we are, and to become what we are capable of becoming, is the only end of life. It is "when we fall behind ourselves" that "we are cursed with duties and the neglect of duties." "I love the wild," he says, "not less than the good." And again: "The life of a good man will hardly improve us more than the life of a free-booter, for the inevitable laws appear as plainly in the infringement as in the observance, and" (mark this) *"our lives are sustained by a nearly equal expense of virtue of some kind."* Even although he were a prig, it will be owned he could announce a startling doctrine. "As for doing good," he writes elsewhere, "that is one of the professions that are full. Moreover, I have tried it fairly, and, strange as it may seem, am satisfied that it does not agree with my constitution. Probably I should not conscientiously and deliberately forsake my particular calling to do the good which society demands of me, to save the universe from annihilation; and I believe that a like but infinitely greater steadfastness elsewhere is all that now preserves it. If you should ever be betrayed into any of these philanthropies, do not let your left hand know what your right hand does, for it is not worth knowing." Elsewhere he returns upon the subject, and explains his meaning thus: "If I ever *did* a man any good in their sense, of course it was something exceptional and insignificant compared with the good or evil I am constantly doing by being what I am." There is a rude nobility, like that of a barbarian king, in this unshaken confidence in himself and indifference to the wants, thoughts, or sufferings of others. In the whole man I find no trace of pity. This was partly the result of theory, for he held the world too mysterious to be criticised, and asks conclusively: "What right have I to grieve who have not ceased to wonder?" But it sprang still more from constitutional indifference and superiority; and he grew up healthy, composed, and unconscious from among life's horrors, like a green bay tree from a field of battle. It was from this lack in himself that he failed to do justice to the spirit of Christ; for while he could glean more meaning from individual precepts than any score of Christians, yet he conceived life in such a different hope, and viewed it with such contrary emotions, that the sense and purport of the doctrine as a whole seems to have passed him by or left him unimpressed. He could understand the idealism of the Christian view, but he was himself so unaffectedly unhuman that he did not recognize the human intention and essence of that teaching. Hence he complained that Christ did not leave us a rule that was proper and sufficient for this world, not having conceived the nature of the rule that was laid down; for things of that character that are sufficiently unacceptable become positively nonexistent to the mind. But perhaps we shall best appreciate the defect in Thoreau by seeing it supplied in the case of Whitman. For the one, I feel confident, is the disciple of the other; it is what Thoreau clearly whispered that Whitman so uproariously bawls; it is the same doctrine, but with how immense a difference! the same argument, but used to what a new conclusion!

Thoreau had plenty of humor until he tutored himself out of it, and so forfeited that best birthright of a sensible man; Whitman, in that respect, seems to have been sent into the world naked and unashamed; and yet by a strange consummation, it is the theory of the former that is arid, abstract, and claustral. Of these two philosophies, so nearly identical at bottom, the one pursues self-improvement—a churlish, mangy dog; the other is up with the morning, in the best of health, and following the nymph Happiness, buxom, blithe, and debonair. Happiness, at least, is not solitary; it joys to communicate; it loves others, for it depends on them for its existence; it sanctions and encourages to all delights that are not unkind in themselves; if it lived to a thousand, it would not make excision of a single humorous passage; and while the self-improver dwindles toward the prig, and, if he be not of an excellent constitution, may even grow deformed into an Obermann, the very name and appearance of a happy man breathe of good nature, and help the rest of us to live.

In the case of Thoreau, so great a show of doctrine demands

some outcome in the field of action. If nothing were to be done but build a shanty beside Walden Pond, we have heard altogether too much of these declarations of independence. That the man wrote some books is nothing to the purpose, for the same has been done in a suburban villa. That he kept himself happy is perhaps a sufficient excuse, but it is disappointing to the reader. We may be unjust, but when a man despises commerce and philanthropy alike, and has views of good so soaring that he must take himself apart from mankind for their cultivation, we will not be content without some striking act. It was not Thoreau's fault if he were not martyred; had the occasion come, he would have made a noble ending. As it is, he did once seek to interfere in the world's course; he made one practical appearance on the stage of affairs; and a strange one it was, and strangely characteristic of the nobility and the eccentricity of the man. It was forced on him by his calm but radical opposition to negro slavery. "Voting for the right is doing nothing for it," he saw; "it is only expressing to men feebly your desire that it should prevail." For his part, he would not "for an instant recognize that political organization for *his.* government which is the slave's government also." "I do not hesitate to say," he adds, "that those who call themselves Abolitionists should at once effectually withdraw their support, both in person and property, from the Government of Massachusetts." That is what he did: in 1843, he ceased to pay the poll-tax. The highway tax he paid, for he said he was as desirous to be a good neighbor as to be a bad subject; but no more poll-tax to the state of Massachusetts. Thoreau had now seceded, and was a polity unto himself; or, as he explains it with admirable sense: "In fact, I quietly declare war with the State after my fashion, though I will still make what use and get what advantage of her I can, as is usual in such cases." He was put in prison; but that was a part of his design. "Under a government which imprisons any unjustly, the true place for a just man is also a prison. I know this well, that if one thousand, if one hundred, if ten men whom I could name—ay, if *one* HONEST man, in this State of Massachusetts, *ceasing to hold slaves,* were actually to withdraw from his copartnership, and be locked in the country jail therefor, it would be the abolition of slavery in America. For it matters not how small the beginning may seem to be; what is once well done is done for ever." Such was his theory of civil disobedience.

And the upshot? A friend paid the tax for him; continued year by year to pay it in the sequel; and Thoreau was free to walk the woods unmolested. It was a fiasco, but to me it does not seem laughable; even those who joined in the laughter at the moment would be insensibly affected by this quaint instance of a good man's horror for injustice. We may compute the worth of that one night's imprisonment as outweighing half a hundred voters at some subsequent election; and if Thoreau had possessed as great a power of persuasion as (let us say) Falstaff, if he had counted a party however small, if his example had been followed by a hundred or by thirty of his fellows, I cannot but believe it would have greatly precipitated the era of freedom and justice. We feel the misdeeds of our country with so little fervor, for we are not witnesses to the suffering they cause; but when we see them wake an active horror in our fellow-man, when we see a neighbor prefer to lie in prison than be so much as passively implicated in their perpetration, even the dullest of us will begin to realize them with a quicker pulse.

Not far from twenty years later, when Captain John Brown was taken at Harper's Ferry, Thoreau was the first to come forward in his defence. The committees wrote to him unanimously that his action was premature. "I did not send to you for advice," said he, "but to announce that I was to speak." I have used the word "defence"; in truth he did not seek to defend him, even declared it would be better for the good cause that he should die; but he praised his action as I think Brown would have liked to hear it praised.

Thus this singularly eccentric and independent mind, wedded to a character of so much strength, singleness, and purity, pursued its own path of self-improvement for more than half a century, part gymnosophist, part backwoodsman; and thus did it come twice . . . into the field of political history.

As Stevenson tells us, he later made an about-face in his opinion of Thoreau. Unfortunately, his recantation, which he appended to later editions of the essay in book form, is almost completely unknown.

STEVENSON'S RECANTATION

Here is an admirable instance of the "point of view" forced throughout, and of too earnest reflection on imperfect facts. Upon me this pure, narrow, sunnily-ascetic Thoreau had exercised a great charm. I have scarce written ten sentences since I was introduced to him, but his influence might be somewhere detected by a close observer. Still it was as a writer that I had made his acquaintance; I took him on his own explicit terms; and when I learned details of his life, they were, by the nature of the case and my own *parti-pris,* read even with a certain violence in terms of his writings. There could scarce be a perversion more justifiable than that; yet it was still a perversion. The study, indeed, raised so much ire in the breast of Dr. Japp (H. A. Page), Thoreau's sincere and learned disciple, that had either of us been men, I please myself with thinking, of less temper and justice, the difference might have made us enemies instead of making us friends. To him who knew the man from the inside, many of my statements sounded like inversions made on purpose; and yet when we came to talk of them together, and he had understood how I was looking at the man through the books, while he had long since learned to read the books through the man, I believe he understood the spirit in which I had been led astray.

On two most important points, Dr. Japp added to my knowledge, and with the same blow fairly demolished that part of my criticism. First, if Thoreau were content to dwell by Walden Pond,

From *Familiar Studies of Men and Books* (London: Chatto and Windus, 1886).

it was not merely with designs of self-improvement, but to serve mankind in the highest sense. Hither came the fleeing slave; thence was he despatched along the road to freedom. That shanty in the woods was a station in the great Underground Railroad; that adroit and philosophic solitary was an ardent worker, soul and body, in that so much more than honorable movement, which, if atonement were possible for nations, should have gone far to wipe away the guilt of slavery. But in history sin always meets with condign punishment; the generation passes, the offence remains, and the innocent must suffer. No underground railroad could atone for slavery, even as no bills in Parliament can redeem the ancient wrongs of Ireland. But here at least is a new light shed on the Walden episode.

Second, it appears, and the point is capital, that Thoreau was once fairly and manfully in love, and, with perhaps too much aping of the angel, relinquished the woman to his brother. Even though the brother were like to die of it, we have not yet heard the last opinion of the woman. But be that as it may, we have here the explanation of the "rarefied and freezing air" in which I complained that he had taught himself to breathe. Reading the man through the books, I took his professions in good faith. He made a dupe of me, even as he was seeking to make a dupe of himself, wrestling philosophy to the needs of his own sorrow. But in the light of this new fact, those pages, seemingly so cold, are seen to be alive with feeling. What appeared to be a lack of interest in the philosopher turns out to have been a touching insincerity of the man to his own heart; and that fine-spun airy theory of friendship, so devoid, as I complained, of any quality of flesh and blood, a mere anodyne to lull his pains. The most temperate of living critics once marked a passage of my own with a cross and the words, "This seems nonsense." It not only seemed; it was so. It was a private bravado of my own, which I had so often repeated to keep up my spirits, that I had grown at last wholly to believe it, and had ended by setting it down as a contribution to the theory of life. So with the more icy parts of this philosophy of Thoreau's. He was affecting the Spartanism he had not; and the old sentimental wound still bled afresh, while he deceived himself with reasons.

Thoreau's theory, in short, was one thing and himself another: of the first, the reader will find what I believe to be a pretty faithful statement and a fairly just criticism in the study; of the second he will find but a contorted shadow. So much of the man as fitted nicely with his doctrines, in the photographer's phrase came out. But that large part which lay outside and beyond, for which he had found or sought no formula, on which perhaps his philosophy even looked askance, is wanting in my study, as it was wanting in the guide I followed. In some ways a less serious writer, in all ways a nobler man, the true Thoreau still remains to be depicted.

[1881]

John Burroughs wrote frequently on Thoreau. Here he points out quite rightly that Thoreau was more interested in natural philosophy than natural science. In later years he forgot that and devoted most of his criticism to pointing out Thoreau's many errors in scientific identification of species, and thus lost the broader concept of Thoreau's work.

THOREAU'S WILDNESS

BY JOHN BURROUGHS

Doubtless the wildest man New England has turned out since the red aborigines vacated her territory was Henry Thoreau,—a man in whom the Indian reappeared on the plane of taste and morals. One is tempted to apply to him his own lines on "Elisha Dugan," as it is very certain they fit himself much more closely than they ever did his neighbors:—

> "O man of wild habits,
> Partridges and rabbits,
> Who hast no cares,
> Only to set snares,
> Who liv'st all alone
> Close to the bone,
> And where life is sweetest
> Constantly eatest."

His whole life was a search for the wild, not only in nature but in literature, in life, in morals. The shyest and most elusive thoughts and impressions were the ones that fascinated him most, not only in his own mind, but in the minds of others. His startling paradoxes are only one form his wildness took. He cared little for science,

From *Critic*, I (March 26, 1881), 74-75.

except as it escaped the rules and technicalities, and put him on the trail of the ideal, the transcendental. Thoreau was of French extraction; and every drop of his blood seems to have turned toward the aboriginal, as the French blood has so often done in other ways in this country. He, for the most part, despised the white man; but his enthusiasm kindled at the mention of the Indian. He envied the Indian; he coveted his knowledge, his arts, his woodcraft. He accredited him with a more "practical and vital science" than was contained in the books. "The Indian stood nearer to wild Nature than we." "It was a new light when my guide gave me Indian names for things for which I had only scientific ones before. In proportion as I understood the language, I saw them from a new point of view." And again, "The Indian's earthly life was as far off from us as Heaven is." In his "Week" he complains that our poetry is only white man's poetry. "If we could listen but for an instant to the chant of the Indian muse, we should understand why he will not exchange his savageness for civilization." Speaking of himself, he says, "I am convinced that my genius dates from an older era than the agricultural. I would at least strike my spade into the earth with such careless freedom, but accuracy, as the woodpecker his bill into a tree. There is in my nature, methinks, a singular yearning toward all wildness." Again and again he returns to the Indian. "We talk of civilizing the Indian, but that is not the name for his improvement. By the wary independence and aloofness of his dim forest life he preserves his intercourse with his native gods, and is admitted from time to time to a rare and peculiar society with Nature. He has glances of starry recognition, to which our saloons are strangers. The steady illumination of his genius, dim only because distant, is like the faint but satisfying light of the stars compared with the dazzling but ineffectual and short-lived blaze of candles." "We would not always be soothing and taming nature, breaking the horse and the ox, but sometimes ride the horse wild, and chase the buffalo." The only relics that interest him are Indian relics. One of his regular spring recreations or occupations is the hunting of arrow-heads. "I spend many hours every spring," he says, "gath-

ering the crop which the melting snow and rain have washed bare.
When, at length, some island in the meadow or some sandy field
elsewhere has been ploughed, perhaps for rye, in the fall, I take
note of it, and do not fail to repair thither as soon as the earth
begins to be dry in the spring. If the spot chances never to have
been cultivated before, I am the first to gather a crop from it. The
farmer little thinks that another reaps a harvest which is the fruit
of his toil." He probably picked up thousands of arrow-heads. He
had an eye for them. The Indian in him recognized its own.

His genius itself is arrow-like, and typical of the wild weapon he
so loved,—hard, flinty, fine-grained, penetrating, winged, a flying
shaft, bringing down its game with marvelous sureness. His literary
art was to let fly with a kind of quick inspiration; and though his
arrows sometimes go wide, yet it is always a pleasure to watch their
aerial course. Indeed, Thoreau was a kind of Emersonian or transcendental red man, going about with a pocket-glass and an
herbarium, instead of with a bow and a tomahawk. He appears to
have been as stoical and indifferent and unsympathetic as a
veritable Indian; and how he hunted without trap or gun, and
fished without hook or snare! Everywhere the wild drew him.
He liked the telegraph because it was a kind of aeolian harp; the
wind blowing upon it made wild, sweet music. He liked the railroad
through his native town, because it was the wildest road he
knew of: it only made deep cuts into and through the hills.
"On it are no houses for foot-travelers. The travel on it does
not disturb me. The woods are left to hang over it. Though
straight, it is wild in its accompaniments, keeping all its raw
edges. Even the laborers on it are not like other laborers."
One day he passed a little boy in the street who had on a home-
made cap of woodchuck's skin, and it completely filled his eye.
He makes a delightful note about it in his journal. That was the
kind of cap to have,—"a perfect little idyl, as they say." Any wild
trait unexpectedly cropping out in any of the domestic animals
pleased him immensely. . . .

Thoreau hesitated to call himself a naturalist. That was too
tame; he would perhaps have been content to have been an Indian

naturalist. He says in this journal, and with much truth and force, "Man cannot afford to be a naturalist, to look at Nature directly, but only with the side of his eye. He must look through and beyond her. To look at her is as fatal as to look at the head of Medusa. It turns the man of science to stone." When he was applied to by the secretary of the Association for the Advancement of Science, at Washington, for information as to the particular branch of science he was most interested in, he confesses he was ashamed to answer for fear of exciting ridicule. But he says, "If it had been the secretary of an association of which Plato or Aristotle was the president, I should not have hesitated to describe my studies at once and particularly." "The fact is, I am a mystic, a transcendentalist, and a natural philosopher to boot." Indeed, what Thoreau was finally after in nature was something ulterior to poetry, something ulterior to philosophy; it was that vague something which he calls "the higher law," and which eludes all direct statement. He went to Nature as to an oracle; and though he sometimes, indeed very often, questioned her as a naturalist and a poet, yet there was always another question in his mind. He ransacked the country about Concord in all seasons and weathers, and at all times of the day and night he delved into the ground, he probed the swamps, he searched the waters, he dug into woodchuck holes, into muskrats' dens, into the retreats of the mice and squirrels; he saw every bird, heard every sound, found every wild-flower, and brought home many a fresh bit of natural history; but he was always searching for something he did not find. This search of his for the transcendental, the unfindable, the wild that will not be caught, he has set forth in a beautiful parable in "Walden:"—

"I long ago lost a hound, a bay horse, and a turtle-dove, and am still on their trail. Many are the travellers I have spoken concerning them, describing their tracks, and what calls they answered to. I have met one or two who had heard the hound, and the tramp of the horse, and even seen the dove disappear behind a cloud; and they seemed as anxious to recover them as if they had lost them themselves."

[1890]

When in 1890 the English psychologist wrote a chapter on Whitman in his The New Spirit, *he devoted a surprisingly large portion of the essay to Thoreau. It is quite probable that this interest in the Concordian stems from Ellis' friendship with Henry Salt, who in that same year issued his first biography of Thoreau. Like Salt, Ellis was one of the pioneers in approaching Thoreau as a thinker as well as a naturalist.*

THOREAU

BY HAVELOCK ELLIS

... Thoreau, an original and solitary spirit, born amid the same influences as Emerson, but of different temperament, resolved to go out into the world, to absorb Nature and the health of Nature: "I wished to live deliberately, to front only the essential facts of life, and see if I could not learn what it had to teach, and not, when I came to die, discover that I had not lived. I did not wish to live what was not life, living is so dear; nor did I wish to practice resignation, unless it was quite necessary. I wanted to live deep and suck out all the marrow of life, to live so sturdily and Spartanlike as to put to rout all that was not life, to cut a broad swath and shave close, to drive life into a corner and reduce it to its lowest terms." So he went into Walden Woods and built himself a hut, and sowed beans, and grew strangely familiar with the lives of plants and trees, of birds and beasts and fishes, and with much else besides. This period of self-dependent residence by Walden Pond has usually been regarded as the chief episode in Thoreau's

---

The New Spirit (London: George Bell & Sons, 1890), pp. 90-99.

91

life. Doubtless it was, in the case of a man who spent his whole life in a small New England town, and made the very moderate living that he needed by intermittent work at pencil-making, teaching, land-surveying, magazine-writing, fence-building, or whitewashing. Certainly it was this experience which gave form and character to the activities of his life, and the book in which he recorded his experiences created his fame. But in the experience itself there was nothing of heroic achievement. One would rather say that in the Walden episode Thoreau has vindicated the place of such an experience in all education. Every one, for some brief period in early life, should be thrown on his own resources in the solitudes of Nature, to enter into harmonious relations with himself, and to realize the full scope of self-reliance. For the man or woman to whom this experience has never been given, the world must hold many needless mysteries and not a few needless miseries.

There was in this man a curious mingling of wildness and austerity, which Mr. Burroughs, in the most discriminating estimate of him yet made, traces to his ancestry. On the paternal side he was French; his privateering grandfather came from Jersey: "that wild revolutionary cry of his, and that sort of restrained ferocity and hirsuteness are French." But on the mother's side he was of Scotch and New England Puritan stock. In person he was rather undersized, with "huge Emersonian nose," and deep-set bluish-gray eyes beneath large over-hanging brows; prominent pursed-up lips, a weak receding chin, "a ruddy weather-beaten face, which reminds one of some shrewd and honest animal's." He was a vigorous pedestrian; he had sloping shoulders, long arms, short legs, large hands and feet—the characteristics, for the most part, of an anthropoid ape. His hands were frequently clenched, and there was an air of concentrated energy about him; otherwise nothing specially notable, and he was frequently supposed "a peddler of small wares." He possessed, as his friend Emerson remarked, powers of observation which seemed to indicate additional senses: "he saw as with microscope, heard as with ear-trumpet, and his memory was a photographic register of all he saw and heard."

It has been claimed for Thoreau by some of his admirers, never by himself, that he was a man of science, a naturalist. His peculiar powers of observation, and habits of noting and recording natural facts, his patience, his taste for spending his days and nights in the open air, seem to furnish everything that is required. Nor would his morbid dislike of dissection have been any serious bar, for the least worked but by no means the least important portion of natural history is the study of living forms, and for this Thoreau seems to have been peculiarly adapted; he had acquired one of the rarest of arts, that of approaching birds, beasts and fishes, and exciting no fear. There are all sorts of profoundly interesting investigations which only such a man can profitably undertake. But that right question which is at least the half of knowledge was hidden from Thoreau; he seems to have been absolutely deficient in scientific sense. His bare, impersonal records of observations are always dull and unprofitable reading; occasionally he stumbles on a good observation but, not realizing its significance, he never verifies it or follows it up. His science is that of a fairly intelligent schoolboy—a counting of birds' eggs and a running after squirrels. Of the vital and organic relationships of facts, or even of the existence of such relationships, he seems to have no perception. Compare any of his books with, for instance, Belt's "Naturalist in Nicaragua," or any of Wallace's books: for the men of science, in their spirit of illuminating inquisitiveness, all facts are instructive; in Thoreau's hands they are all dead. He was not a naturalist: he was an artist and a moralist.

He was born into an atmosphere of literary culture, and the great art he cultivated was that of framing sentences. He desired to make sentences which would "suggest far more than they say," which would "lie like bowlders on the page, up and down or across, not mere repetition, but creation, and which a man might sell his ground or cattle to build," sentences "as durable as a Roman aqueduct." Undoubtedly he succeeded; his sentences frequently have all the massive and elemental qualities of style. There is a keen exhilarating breeze blowing about these bowlders, and when we look at them they have the grace and audacity, the happy, natural extravagance of fragments of the finest Decorated Gothic on the site of a fourteenth century abbey. He was in love with the things that are wildest and most untamable in Nature, and of these his sentences often seem to be a solid artistic embodiment, the mountain side, "its sublime gray mass, that antique, brownish-gray, Ararat color," or the "ancient, familiar, immortal cricket sound," the thrush's song, his *ranz des vâches,* or the song that of all seemed to rejoice him most, the clear, exhilarating, braggart, clarion-crow of the cock. Thoreau's favorite reading was among the Greeks, Pindar, Simonides, the Greek Anthology, especially Æschylus, and a later ancient, Milton. There is something of his paganism in all this, his cult of the aboriginal health-bearing forces of Nature. His paganism, however unobtrusive, was radical and genuine. It was a paganism much earlier than Plato, and which had never heard of Christ.

Thoreau was of a piece; he was at harmony with himself, though it may be that the elements that went to make up the harmony were few. The austerity and exhilaration and simple paganism of his art were at one with his morality. He was, at the very core, a preacher; the morality that he preached, interesting in itself, is, for us, the most significant thing about him. Thoreau was, in the noblest sense of the word, a cynic. The school of Antisthenes is not the least interesting of the Socratic schools, and Thoreau is perhaps the finest flower that that school has ever yielded. He may not have been aware of his affinities, but it will help us if we bear them in mind. The charm that Diogenes exercised over men seems to have consisted in his peculiarly fresh and original intellect, his extravagant independence and self-control, his coarse and effective wit. Thoreau sat in his jar at Walden with the same originality, independence, and sublime contentment; but his wisdom was suave and his wit was never coarse—exalted, rather, into a perennial humor, flashing now and then into divine epigram. A life in harmony with Nature, the culture of joyous simplicity, the subordination of science to ethics—these were the principles of cynicism, and to these Thoreau was always true. "Every day is a festival," said Diogenes, and Metrocles rejoiced that he was happier than the Persian king. "I would rather sit on a pumpkin and have it all to myself," said Thoreau, "than be crowded on a velvet cushion." "Cultivate poverty like a garden herb, like sage. . . . It is life near the bone, where it is sweetest. . . . Money is not required to buy one necessary of the soul." He had "traveled much in Concord." "Methinks I should be content to sit at the back-door in Concord under the poplar tree for ever." Such utterances as these strewn throughout Thoreau's pages—and the saying in the last days of the dying man to the youth who would talk to him about a future world, "One world at a time"—are full, in the uncorrupted sense, of the finest Cynicism. Diogenes, seeing a boy drink out of his hand, threw away his cup; Thoreau had an interesting mineral specimen as a parlor ornament, but it needed dusting every day, and he threw it away: it was not worth its keep. The Cynics seem to have been the first among the Greeks to declare that slavery is opposed to nature. Thoreau not only carried his independence so far as to go to prison rather than pay taxes to Church or State—"the only government that I recognize is the power that establishes justice in the land"—but in 1859, when John Brown lay in prison in Virginia, Thoreau was the one man in America to recognize the greatness of the occasion and to stand up publicly on his side: "Think of him!—of his rare qualities!— such a man as it takes ages to make, and ages to understand; no mock hero, nor the representative of any party. A man such as the sun may not rise upon again in this benighted land. To whose making went the costliest material, the finest adamant; sent to be the redeemer of those in captivity; and the only use to which you can put him is to hang him at the end of a rope!"

Every true Cynic is, above all, a moralist and a preacher. Thoreau could never be anything else; that was, in the end, his greatest weakness. This unfailing ethereality, this perpetual challenge of the acridity and simplicity of Nature, becomes at least hypernatural. Thoreau breakfasts on the dawn: it is well; but he dines on the rainbow and sups on the aurora borealis. Of Nature's treasure more than half is man. Thoreau, with his noble Cynicism, had, as he thought, driven life into a corner, but he had to confess that of all phenomena his own race was to him the most mysterious and undiscoverable. He writes finely: "The whole duty of man may be expressed in one line: Make to yourself a perfect body;" but this appears to be a purely intellectual intuition. He had a fine insight into the purity of sex and of all natural animal functions, from which we excuse ourselves of speaking by falsely saying they are trifles. "We are so degraded that we cannot speak simply of the necessary functions of human nature;" but he is not bold to justify his insight. He welcomed Walt Whitman, at the very first, as the greatest democrat the world had seen, but he himself remained a natural aristocrat. "He was a man devoid of compassion," remarks Mr. Burroughs, "devoid of sympathy, devoid of generosity, devoid of patriotism, as those words are generally understood." He had learnt something of the mystery of Nature, but the price of his knowledge was ignorance of his fellows. The chief part of life he left untouched.

Yet all that he had to give he gave fully and ungrudgingly; and it was of the best and rarest. We shall not easily exhaust the exhilaration of it. "We need the tonic of wildness." Thoreau has heightened for us the wildness of Nature, and his work—all written, as we need not be told, in the open air—is full of this tonicity; it is a sort of moral quinine, and, like quinine under certain circumstances, it leaves a sweet taste behind. . . .

[1901]

*When More graduated from college, he retired to a dilapidated
little farmhouse near Shelburne, New Hampshire, for two years
and there started his widely influential series of Shelburne Essays,
of which this is one of the earliest. He thus criticizes Thoreau
from a Walden of his own. In later years More was one of the
leaders of the Humanist movement.*

A HERMIT'S NOTES ON THOREAU

BY PAUL ELMER MORE

. . . Several times I had read the *Odyssey* within sight of the sea;
and the murmur of the waves on the beach, beating through the
rhythm of the poem, had taught me how vital a thing a book might
be, and how it could acquire a peculiar validity from harmonious
surroundings; but now the reading of Thoreau in that charmed
and lonely spot emphasized this commonplace truth in a special
manner. *Walden* studied in the closet, and *Walden* mused over
under the trees, by running water, are two different books. And
then, from Thoreau, the greatest by far of our writers on Nature,
and the creator of a new sentiment in literature, my mind turned
to the long list of Americans who have left, or are still composing,
a worthy record of their love and appreciation of the natural
world. Our land of multiform activities has produced so little that
is really creative in literature or art! Hawthorne and Poe, and
possibly one or two others, were masters in their own field; yet
even they chose not quite the highest realm for their genius to

From *Atlantic Monthly*, LXXXVII (June, 1901), 857-64. A lengthy introduction
has been deleted, as well as two digressions within the essay.

work in. But in one subject our writers have led the way and are still preeminent: Thoreau was the creator of a new manner of writing about Nature. In its deeper essence his work is inimitable, as it is the voice of a unique personality; but in its superficial aspects it has been taken up by a host of living writers, who have caught something of his method, even if they lack his genius and singleness of heart. From these it was an easy transition to compare Thoreau's attitude of mind with that of Wordsworth and the other great poets of his century who went to Nature for their inspiration, and made Nature-writing the characteristic note of modern verse. What is it in Thoreau that is not to be found in Byron and Shelley and Wordsworth, not to mention old Izaak Walton, Gilbert White of Selborne, and a host of others? It was a rare treat, as I lay in that leafy covert, to go over in memory the famous descriptive passages from these authors, and to contrast their spirit with that of the book in my hand.

As I considered these matters, it seemed to me that Thoreau's work was distinguished from that of his American predecessors and imitators by just these qualities of awe and wonder which we, in our communings with Nature, so often cast away. Mere description, though it may at times have a scientific value, is after all a very cheap form of literature; and, as I have already intimated, too much curiosity of detail is likely to exert a deadening influence on the philosophic and poetic contemplation of Nature. Such an influence is, as I believe, specially noticeable at the present time, and even Thoreau was not entirely free from its baneful effect. Much of his writing, perhaps the greater part, is the mere record of observation and classification, and has not the slightest claim on our remembrance,—unless, indeed, it possesses some scientific value, which I doubt. Certainly the parts of his work having permanent interest are just those chapters where he is less the minute observer, and more the contemplative philosopher. Despite the width and exactness of his information, he was far from having the truly scientific spirit; the acquisition of knowledge, with him, was in the end quite subordinate to his interest in the moral significance of Nature, and the words he read in her obscure scroll were a language of strange mysteries, oftentimes of awe. It is a constant reproach to the prying, self-satisfied habits of small minds to see the reverence of this great-hearted observer before the supreme goddess he so loved and studied. Much of this contemplative spirit of Thoreau is due to the soul of the man himself, to that personal force which no analysis of character can explain. But, besides this, it has always seemed to me that, more than in any other descriptive writer of the land, his mind is the natural outgrowth, and his essays the natural expression, of a feeling deep-rooted in the historical beginnings of New England; and this foundation in the past gives a strength and convincing force to his words that lesser writers utterly lack.

. . . It is this New World inheritance, moreover,—joined, of course, with his own inexplicable personality, which must not be left out of account,—that makes Thoreau's attitude toward Nature something quite distinct from that of the great poets who just preceded him. There was in him none of the fiery spirit of the revolution which caused Byron to mingle hatred of men with enthusiasm for the Alpine solitudes. There was none of the passion for beauty and the voluptuous self-abandonment of Keats; these were not in the atmosphere he breathed at Concord. He was not touched with Shelley's unearthly mysticism, nor had he ever fed

> on the aerial kisses
> Of shapes that haunt thought's wildernesses;

his moral sinews were too stark and strong for that form of mental dissipation. Least of all did he, after the manner of Wordsworth, hear in the voice of Nature any compassionate plea for the weakness and sorrow of the downtrodden. Philanthropy and humanitarian sympathies were to him a desolation and a woe. "Philanthropy is almost the only virtue which is sufficiently appreciated by mankind. Nay, it is greatly overrated; and it is our selfishness which overrates it," he writes. And again: "The philanthropist too often surrounds mankind with the remembrance of his own cast-off griefs as an atmosphere, and calls it sympathy." Similarly his reliance on the human will was too sturdy to be much perturbed by the inequalities and sufferings of mankind, and his faith in the individual was too unshaken to be led into humanitarian interest in the masses. "Alas! this is the crying sin of the age," he declares, "this want of faith in the prevalence of a man."

But the deepest and most essential difference is the lack of pantheistic reverie in Thoreau. It is this brooding over the universal spirit embodied in the material world which almost always marks the return of sympathy with Nature, and which is particularly noticeable in the writers of the past century.

. . . Of all this pantheism, whether attended with revolt from responsibility or languid reverie or humanitarian dreams, there is hardly a trace in Thoreau. The memory of man's struggle with the primeval woods and fields was not so lost in antiquity that the world had grown into an indistinguishable part of human life. If Nature smiled upon Thoreau at times, she was still an alien creature who succumbed only to his force and tenderness, as she had before given her bounty, though reluctantly, to the Pilgrim Fathers. A certain championship he had with the plants and wild beasts of the field, a certain intimacy with the dumb earth; but he did not seek to merge his personality in their impersonal life, or look to them for a response to his own inner moods; he associated with them as the soul associates with the body.

More characteristic is his sense of awe, even of dread, toward the great unsubdued forces of the world. The loneliness of the mountains such as they appeared to the early adventurers in a strange, unexplored country; the repellent loneliness of the barren heights frowning down inhospitably upon the pioneer who scratched the soil at their base; the loneliness and terror of the dark, untrodden forests, where the wanderer might stray away and be lost forever, where savage men were more feared than the wild animals, and where superstition saw the haunt of the Black Man and of all uncleanness,—all this tradition of sombre solitude made Nature to Thoreau something very different from the hills and valleys of Old England. "We have not seen pure Nature," he says, "unless we have seen her thus vast and drear and inhuman. . . . Man was not to be associated with it. It was matter, vast, terrific,—

not his Mother Earth that we have heard of, not for him to tread on, or be buried in,—no, it were being too familiar even to let his bones lie there,—the home, this, of Necessity and Fate." After reading Byron's invocation to the Alps as the palaces of Nature; or the ethereal mountain scenes in Shelley's *Alastor,* where all the sternness of the everlasting hills is dissolved into rainbow hues of shifting light as dainty as the poet's own soul; or Wordsworth's familiar musings in the vale of Grasmere,—if, after these, we turn to Thoreau's account of the ascent of Mount Katahdin, we seem at once to be in the home of another tradition. I am tempted to quote a few sentences of that account to emphasize the point. On the mountain heights, he says of the beholder:

> He is more lone than you can imagine. There is less of substantial thought and fair understanding in him than in the plains where men inhabit. His reason is dispersed and shadowy, more thin and subtle, like the air. Vast, Titanic, inhuman Nature has got him at disadvantage, caught him alone, and pilfers him of some of his divine faculty. She does not smile on him as in the plains. She seems to say sternly, Why came ye here before your time? This ground is not prepared for you. Is it not enough that I smile in the valleys? I have never made this soil for thy feet, this air for thy breathing, these rocks for thy neighbors. I cannot pity nor fondle thee here, but forever relentlessly drive thee hence to where I *am* kind.

I do not mean to present the work of Thoreau as equal in value to the achievement of the great poets with whom I have compared him, but wish merely in this way to bring out more definitely his characteristic traits. Yet if his creative genius is less than theirs, I cannot but think his attitude toward Nature is in many respects truer and more wholesome. Pantheism, whether on the banks of the Ganges or of the Thames, seems to bring with it a spreading taint of effeminacy; and from this the mental attitude of our Concord naturalist was eminently free. There is something tonic and bracing in his intercourse with the rude forces of the forest; he went to Walden Pond because he had "private business to transact," not for relaxation and mystical reverie. "To be a philosopher," he said, "is not merely to have subtle thoughts, nor even to found a school, but so to love wisdom as to live according to its dictates, a life of simplicity, independence, magnanimity, and trust;" and by recurring to the solitudes of Nature he thought he could best develop in himself just these manly virtues. Nature was to him a discipline of the will as much as a stimulant to the imagination. He would, if it were possible, "combine the hardiness of the savages with the intellectualness of the civilized man;" and in this method of working out the philosophical life we see again the influence of long and deep-rooted tradition. To the first settlers, the red man was as much an object of curiosity and demanded as much study as the earth they came to cultivate; their books are full of graphic pictures of savage life, and it should seem as if now in Thoreau this inherited interest had received at last its ripest expression. When he travelled in the wilderness of Maine, he was as much absorbed in learning the habits of his Indian guides as in exploring the woods. He had some innate sympathy or perception which taught him to find relics of old Indian life where others would pass them by, and there is a well-known story of his answer to one who asked him where such relics could be discovered: he merely stooped down and picked an arrowhead from the ground.

And withal his stoic virtues never dulled his sense of awe, and his long years of observation never lessened his feeling of strangeness in the presence of solitary Nature. If at times his writing descends into the cataloguing style of the ordinary naturalist, yet the old tradition of wonder was too strong in him to be more than temporarily obscured. Unfortunately, his occasional faults have become in some of his recent imitators the staple of their talent: but Thoreau was pre-eminently the poet and philosopher of his school, and I cannot do better than close these desultory notes with . . . a passage which seems to me to convey most vividly his sensitiveness to the solemn mystery of the deep forest:

> We heard [he writes in his Chesuncook], come faintly echoing, or creeping from afar, through the moss-clad aisles, a dull, dry, rushing sound, with a solid core to it, yet as if half smothered under the grasp of the luxuriant and fungus-like forest, like the shutting of a door in some distant entry of the damp and shaggy wilderness. If we had not been there, no mortal had heard it. When we asked Joe [the Indian guide] in a whisper what it was, he answered, — "Tree fall."

[1908]

*It is unfortunate that there are not more essays on Thoreau's in-
dividual works written with the authority of Mrs. Eckstorm's essay.
She spent more than eighty years of her life living in Bangor, the
gateway to the Maine Woods. The daughter of a lumberman who
had worked these woods with Thoreau's trip companion George
Thatcher, she was unquestionably the pre-eminent authority on his
Maine writings.*

THOREAU'S "MAINE WOODS"

BY FANNIE HARDY ECKSTORM

It is more than half a century since Henry D. Thoreau made
his last visit to Maine. And now the forest which he came to see
has all but vanished, and in its place stands a new forest with new
customs. No one should expect to find here precisely what Thoreau
found; therefore, before all recollection of the old days has passed
away, it is fitting that some one who knew their traditions should
bear witness to Thoreau's interpretation of the Maine woods.

We hardly appreciate how great are the changes of the last fifty
years; how the steamboat, the motor-boat, the locomotive, and
even the automobile, have invaded regions which twenty years
ago could be reached only by the lumberman's batteau and the
hunter's canoe; how cities have arisen, and more are being pro-
jected, on the same ground where Thoreau says that "the best
shod travel for the most part with wet feet," and that "melons,
squashes, sweet-corn, tomatoes, beans, and many other vegetables,
could not be ripened," because the forest was so dense and moist.

From *Atlantic Monthly*, CII (August, 1908), 242-50.

Less than twenty years since there was not a sporting camp in any part of the northern Maine wilderness; now who may number them? Yet, even before the nineties, when one could travel for days and meet no one, the pine tree was gone; the red-shirted lumberman was gone; the axe was about to give place to the saw; and soon, almost upon the clearing where Thoreau reported the elder Fowler, the remotest settler, as wholly content in his solitude and thinking that "neighbors, even the best, were only trouble and expense," was to rise one of the largest pulp mills in the world, catching the logs midway their passage down the river and grinding them into paper. And the pine tree, of which Thoreau made so much? Native to the state and long accustomed to its woods, I cannot remember ever having seen a perfect, old-growth white pine tree; it is doubtful if there is one standing in the state to-day.

So the hamadryad has fled before the demand for ship-timber and Sunday editions, and the unblemished forest has passed beyond recall. There are woods enough still; there is game enough,—more of some kinds than in the old days; there are fish enough; there seems to be room enough for all who come; but the man who has lived here long realizes that the woods are being "camped to death;" and the man who is old enough to remember days departed rustles the leaves of Thoreau's book when he would listen again to the pine tree soughing in the wind.

What is it that *The Maine Woods* brings to us besides? The moods and music of the forest; the vision of white tents beside still waters; of canoes drawn out on pebbly beaches; of camp-fires flickering across rippling rapids; the voice of the red squirrels, "spruce and fine;" the melancholy laughter of the loon, and the mysterious "night warbler," always pursued and never apprehended. Most of all it introduces us to Thoreau himself.

It must be admitted in the beginning that *The Maine Woods* is not a masterpiece. Robert Louis Stevenson discards it as not literature. It is, however, a very good substitute, and had Robert Louis worn it next to the skin he might perhaps have absorbed enough of the spirit of the American forest to avoid the gaudy melodrama which closes *The Master of Ballantrae*. *The Maine Woods* is of another world. Literature it may not be, nor one of "the three books of his that will be read with much pleasure;" but it is—the Maine woods. Since Thoreau's day, whoever has looked at these woods to advantage has to some extent seen them through Thoreau's eyes. Certain it is that no other man has ever put the coniferous forest between the leaves of a book.

For that he came—for that and the Indian. Open it where you will—and the little old first edition is by all odds to be chosen if one is fastidious about the printed page, to get the full savor of it; open where you will and these two speak to you. He finds water "too civilizing;" he wishes to become "selvaggia;" he turns woodworm in his metamorphosis, and loves to hear himself crunching nearer and nearer to the heart of the tree. He is tireless in his efforts to wrench their secrets from the woods; and, in every trial, he endeavors, not to talk *about* them, but to flash them with lightning vividness into the mind of the reader. "It was the opportunity to be ignorant that I improved. It suggested to me that there was something to be seen if one had eyes. It made a believer of me more than before. I believed that the woods were not tenantless, but choke-full of honest spirits as good as myself any day."

It is sometimes the advantage of a second-rate book that it endears the writer to us. The Thoreau of *Walden,* with his housekeeping all opened up for inspection, refusing the gift of a rug rather than shake it, throwing away his paperweight to avoid dusting it—where's the woman believes he *would* have dusted it?—parades his economies priggishly, like some pious anchoret with a business eye fixed on Heaven. But when he tells us in the appendix to the *Woods* that for a cruise three men need only one large knife and one iron spoon (for all), a four-quart tin pail for kettle, two tin dippers, three tin plates and a fry pan, his economy, if extreme, is manly and convincing. We meet him here among men whom we have known ourselves; we see how he treated them and how they treated him, and he appears to better advantage than when skied among the lesser gods of Concord.

Here is Joe Polis, whose judgment of a man would be as shrewd as any mere literary fellow's, and Joe talks freely, which in those days an Indian rarely did with whites. Here is the late Hiram L. Leonard, "the gentlemanly hunter of the stage," known to all anglers by his famous fishing rods. Those who remember his retiring ways will not doubt that it was Thoreau who prolonged the conversation. Here is Deacon George A. Thatcher, the "companion" of the first two trips. That second invitation and the deacon's cordial appreciation of "Henry" bespeak agreeable relations outside those of kinship. The Thoreau whom we meet here smiles at us. We see him, a shortish, squarish, brown-bearded, blue-eyed man, in a check shirt, with a black string tie, thick waistcoat, thick trousers, an old Kossuth hat,—for the costume that he recommends for woods wear must needs have been his own,—and over all a brown linen sack, on which, indelible, is the ugly smutch that he got when he hugged the sooty kettle to his side as he raced Polis across Grindstone Carry.

To every man his own Thoreau! But why is not this laughing runner, scattering boots and tinware, as true to life as any? Brusque, rude, repellant no doubt he often was, and beyond the degree excusable; affecting an unnecessary disdain of the comfortable, harmless goods of life; more proud, like Socrates, of the holes in his pockets than young Alcibiades of his whole, new coat; wrong very often, and most wrong upon his points of pride; yet he still had his southerly side, more open to the sun than to the wind. It is not easy to travel an unstaked course, against the advice and wishes and in the teeth of the prophecies of all one's friends, when it would be sweet and easy to win their approval—and, Himmel! to stop their mouths!—by burning one's faggot. A fighting faith, sleeping on its arms, often has to be stubborn and ungenial. What Henry Thoreau needed was to be believed in through thick and thin, and then let alone; and the very crabbedness, so often complained of, indicates that, like his own wild apples, in order to get a chance to grow, he had to protect himself by thorny underbrush from his too solicitous friends.

There is a popular notion that Thoreau was a great woodsman, able to go anywhere by dark or daylight, without path or guide; that he knew all the secrets of the pioneer and the hunter; that he was unequaled as an observer, and almost inerrant in judgment, being able to determine at a glance weight, measure, distance, area, or cubic contents. The odd thing about these popular opinions is that they are not true. Thoreau was not a woodsman; he was not infallible; he was not a scientific observer; he was not a scientist at all. He could do many things better than most men; but the sum of many excellencies is not perfection.

For the over-estimate of Thoreau's abilities, Emerson is chiefly responsible. His noble eulogy of Thoreau has been misconstrued in a way which shows the alarming aptitude of the human mind for making stupid blunders. We all have a way of taking hold of a striking detail—which Mr. Emerson was a rare one for perceiving—and making of it the whole story. We might name it *the fallacy of the significant detail*. Do we not always see Hawthorne, the youth, walking by night? Who thinks of it as any less habitual than eating his dinner? And because Stevenson, in an unguarded moment, confessed that "he had played the sedulous ape" to certain authors, no writer, out of respect to our weariness, has ever forborne to remind us of that pleasant monkey trick of Stevenson's youth. Nor are we ever allowed to forget that Thoreau "saw as with microscope, heard as with ear-trumpet," and that "his power of observation seemed to indicate additional senses." It is because the majority of mankind see no difference in values between facts aglow with poetic fervor and facts preserved in the cold storage of census reports, that Emerson's splendid eulogy of his friend, with its vivid, personal characterizations rising like the swift bubbles of a boiling spring all through it, has created the unfortunate impression that Thoreau made no blunders.

Emerson himself did not distinguish between the habitual and the accidental; between a clever trick, like that of lifting breams guarding their nests, and the power to handle any kind of fish. He even ran short of available facts, and grouped those of unequal value. To be able to grasp an even dozen of pencils requires but little training; to be able to estimate the weight of a pig, or the cordwood in a tree, needs no more than a fairly good judgment; but that "he could pace sixteen rods more accurately than another man could measure them with rod and chain,"—that is nonsense, for it puts at naught the whole science of surveying. Emerson's data being unequal in rank and kind, the whole sketch is a little out of focus, and consequently the effect is agreeably artistic.

Nor is the matter mended by misquotation. Emerson says, "He could find his path in the woods at night, he said, better by his feet than his eyes." There is nothing remarkable in this. How does any one keep the path across his own lawn on a black dark night? But even so careful a man as Stevenson paraphrases thus: "He could guide himself about the woods on the darkest night by the touch of his feet." Here we have a different matter altogether. By taking out that "path," a very ordinary accomplishment is turned into one quite impossible. Because Emerson lacked woods learning, the least variation from his exact words is likely to result in something as absurd or as exaggerated as this.

Thoreau's abilities have been overrated. *The Maine Woods* contains errors in the estimates of distance, area, speed, and the like, too numerous to mention in detail. No Penobscot boatman can run a batteau over falls at the rate of fifteen miles an hour, as Thoreau says; no canoeman can make a hundred miles a day, even on the St. John River. The best records I can discover fall far short of Thoreau's estimate for an average good day's run. Even when he says that his surveyor's eye thrice enabled him to detect the slope of the current, he magnifies his office. Any woman who can tell when a picture hangs straight can see the slant of the river in all those places.

But his worst error in judgment, and the one most easily appreciated on its own merits, is the error he made in climbing Katahdin. He writes that their camp was "broad off Katahdin and about a dozen miles from the summit," whereas we know that his camp was not five miles in an air-line from the top of the South Slide, and not more than seven from the highest peak. The trail from the stream to the slide has always been called four miles, and Thoreau says that his boatmen told him that it was only four miles to the mountain; "but as I judged, and as it afterwards proved, nearer fourteen." The only reason why it proved "nearer fourteen" was because he did not go the short way. Instead of climbing by the Slide, where all West Branch parties ascend to-day, he laid a northeast course "directly for the base of the highest peak," through all the debris and underbrush at the foot of the mountain, climbing where it is so steep that water hardly dares to run down. He ought to have reasoned that the bare top of a mountain is easy walking, and the nearest practicable point, rather than the peak itself, was the best place to climb.

But surely he was a competent naturalist? There is no space to go over the text in detail, but we may turn directly to the list of birds in the appendix. After making allowance for ornithology in the fifties being one of the inexact sciences, the list must be admitted to be notably bad. It is worse than immediately appears to the student who is not familiar with the older nomenclature. Thoreau names thirty-seven species, and queries four of them as doubtful. Oddly, the most characteristic bird of the region, the Canada jay, which the text mentions as seen, is omitted from the list. Of the doubtful species, the herring gull is a good guess; but the yellow-billed cuckoo and the prairie chicken (of all unlikely guesses the most improbable) are surely errors, while the white-bellied nuthatch, which he did not see, but thought he heard, rests only upon his conjecture. Mr. William Brewster thinks that it might occur in that region in suitably wooded localities, but I can find no record west of Houlton and north of Katahdin. The tree sparrow, though a common migrant, is more than doubtful as summer resident. The pine warbler must be looked upon with equal suspicion. The wood thrush is impossible—a clear mistake for the hermit. His *Fuligula albicola* (error for *albeola*) is not the buffle-headed duck, which breeds north of our limits (and Thoreau was here in July); it is most likely the horned grebe in summer plumage, identified after his return by a picture. Similarly his red-headed woodpecker, which he vouches for thus, "Heard and saw, and good to eat," must have been identified by the vernacular name alone. Among our woodsmen the "red-headed woodpecker" is not *Picus erythrocephalus,* as Thoreau names it, but *Ceophloeus pileatus abieticola,* the great pileated woodpecker, or logcock, a bird twice as large, heavily crested, and wholly different in structure and color. Seven out of the thirty-seven birds are too wrong to be disputed; the white-bellied nuthatch stands on wholly negative evidence; and, if we had fuller data of the forest regions, perhaps several of the others might be challenged.

The list proves that, even according to the feeble light of the day, Thoreau was not an ornithologist. As a botanist he did much better; but that was largely by grace of Gray's *Manual,* then recently published. Of the scientific ardor which works without books and collates and classifies innumerable facts for the sake of systematic knowledge, he had not a particle. His notes, though voluminous and of the greatest interest, rarely furnish material for science. If he examined a partridge chick, newly hatched, it was not to give details of weight and color, but to speculate upon the rare clearness of its gaze. If he recorded a battle between black ants and red, he saw its mock heroic side and wrote an *Antiad* upon the occasion; but he did not wait to see the fight finished, and to count the slain.

It was not as an observer that Thoreau surpassed other men, but as an interpreter. He had the art—and how much of an art it is no one can realize until he has seated himself before an oak or a pine tree and has tried by the hour to write out its equation in terms of humanity—he had the art to see the human values of natural objects, to perceive the ideal elements of unreasoning nature and the service of those ideals to the soul of man. "The greatest delight which the fields and woods minister, is the suggestion of an occult relation between man and the vegetable," wrote Emerson; and it became Thoreau's chief text. It is the philosophy behind Thoreau's words, his attempt to reveal the Me through the Not Me, reversing the ordinary method, which makes his observations of such interest and value.

> Flower in the crannied wall,
> I pluck you out of the crannies; —
> Hold you here, root and all, in my hand,

Little flower — but if I could understand
What you are, root and all, and all in all,
I should know what God and man is.

This power to see is rare; but mere good observation is not super-normal. We must not attribute to Thoreau's eyes what was wrought in his brain; to call him uniquely gifted in matters wherein a thousand men might equal him is not to increase his fame. *The Maine Woods* also shows clearly that Thoreau knew nothing of woodcraft. Do we realize that his longest trip gave him only ten days actually spent in the woods? or that few tourists to-day attempt to cover the same ground in less than two or three weeks? What his own words proclaim there can be no disputing over, and Thoreau admits frankly, and sometimes naively, that he was incapable of caring for himself in the woods, which surely is the least that can be asked of a man to qualify him as a "woodsman."

In the first place, his mind does not work like a woodsman's. "We had not gone far," he writes, "before I was startled by seeing what I thought was an Indian encampment, covered with a red flag, on the bank, and exclaimed 'Camp!' to my comrades. I was slow to discover that it was a red maple changed by the frost." He ought to have been "slow to discover" that it was anything else.

"I could only occasionally perceive his trail in the moss," he writes of Polis, "yet he did not appear to look down nor hesitate an instant, but led us out exactly to the canoe. This surprised me, for without a compass, or the sight or noise of the river to guide us, we could not have kept our course many minutes, and we could have retraced our steps but a short distance, with a great deal of pains and very slowly, using laborious circumspection. But it was evident that he could go back through the forest wherever he had been during the day." A woodsman may have to use "laborious circumspection" in following the trail of another man, but his own he ought to be able to run back without hesitation.

"Often on bare rocky carries," he says again, "the trail was so indistinct that I repeatedly lost it, but when I walked behind him (Polis) I observed that he could keep it almost like a hound, and rarely hesitated, or, if he paused a moment on a bare rock, his eye immediately detected some sign which would have escaped me. Frequently *we* found no path at all in these places, and were to him unaccountably delayed. He would only say it was 'ver strange.' "

"The carry-paths themselves," he says again, "were more than usually indistinct, often the route being revealed only by countless small holes in the fallen timber made by the tacks in the drivers' boots, or where there *was* a slight trail we did not find it." This is almost funny. In those days the carries were little traveled except by the river-drivers; in summer they were much choked with shrubbery; but what did the man expect—a king's highway? That spring the whole East Branch drive, probably a hundred men, had tramped the carry for days; and every man had worn boots each of which, in those days, was armed with twenty-nine inch-long steel spikes. The whole carry had been pricked out like an embroidery pattern. Those little "tack-holes" *were* the carry. If Thoreau could have realized that a river-driver never goes far from water, and that his track is as sure as a mink's or an otter's to lead back to water, he would have appreciated how much, instead of how little, those calkmarks were telling him. But Thoreau did not know the facts of woods life, and when he saw a sign he was often incapable of drawing an inference from it.

The proof that Thoreau did not know the alphabet of wood-craft—if further proof is wanted—is that, on Mud Pond Carry, which, in his day, was the most open and well-trodden of all the woods roads beyond North-East Carry, he took a tote-road, used only for winter hauling, showing neither hoof-mark, sled-track, nor footprint in summer, and left the regular carry, worn by human feet, merely because a sign-board on the former pointed to his ultimate destination, Chamberlain Lake. Now in the woods a tote-road is a tote-road, and a carry is a carry; when a man is told to follow one, he is not expected to turn off upon the other; there is no more reason to confuse the two than to mistake a trolley line for a steam-railroad track. No wonder Polis "thought little of their woodcraft."

But aside from this deficiency in woods education, Thoreau never got to feel at home in the Maine wilderness. He was a good "pasture man," but here was something too large for him. He appreciated all the more its wildness and strangeness; and was the more unready to be venturesome. The very closeness of his acquaintance with Concord conspired to keep him from feeling at home where the surrounding trees, flowers, and birds were largely unfamiliar; for the better a man knows one fauna, the more he is likely to be ill at ease under a different environment. No man has expressed so well the timidity which sometimes assails the stranger when surrounded by the Sabbath peace of the wilderness. "You may penetrate half a dozen rods farther into that twilight wilderness, after some dry bark to kindle your fire with, and wonder what mysteries lie hidden still deeper in it, say at the end of a long day's walk; or you may run down to the shore for a dipper of water, and get a clearer view for a short distance up or down the stream. . . . But there is no sauntering off to see the country, and ten or fifteen rods seems a great way from your companions, and you come back with the air of a much-traveled man, as from a long journey, with adventures to relate, although you may have heard the crackling of the fire all the while,—and at a hundred rods you might be lost past recovery, and have to camp out." That is all very true, but most men do not care to own it. "It was a relief to get back to our smooth and still varied landscape," he writes after a week's trip to Chesuncook, which then, as now, was only the selvage of the woods.

I have a friend of the old school who appreciates Thoreau, but who always balks at one point. "Call him a woodsman!" he cries in disgust; "why, he admits himself that he borrowed the axe that he built his Walden shanty with!" (This seems to him as indefensible as borrowing a toothbrush.)—"But," I urge, "he says, too, that he returned it sharper than when he took it."—"It makes no difference, none at all," says he, "for I tell you that a real woodsman *owns his axe."* The contention is valid; more-over, it is fundamental. A master workman in all trades owns his tools. Those who have praised Thoreau as a woodsman have probably done so under the impression that every man who goes into the woods under the care of a guide is entitled to the name. They have not understood the connotation of the term, and may have even supposed that there is such a thing as an *amateur* woodsman. But there are some few high professions where what-ever is not genuine is counterfeit; half-and-half gentlemen, halting patriots, amateur woodsmen, may safely be set down as no gentlemen, patriots, or woodsmen at all. For in truth woodcraft is a profession which cannot be picked up by browsing in Massa-chusetts pastures, and no one learns it who does not throw himself into it whole-heartedly.

Yet because Thoreau does not measure up to the standard of the woodsman born and bred, it would be wrong to infer that the average city man could have done as well in his place. Well done for an amateur is often not creditable for a professional; but Thoreau's friends demand the honors of a professional. On the other hand, because he made some mistakes in unimportant details, he must not be accused of being unreliable. How trust-worthy Thoreau is may be known by this,—that fifty years after he left the state forever, I can trace out and call by name almost every man whom he even passed while in the woods. He did not know the names of some of them; possibly he did not speak to them; but they can be identified after half a century. And that cannot be done with a slip-shod record of events. The wonder is, not that Thoreau did so little here, but that in three brief visits, a stranger, temperamentally alien to these great wildernesses, he got at the heart of so many matters.

Almost any one can see superficial differences; but to perceive the essence of even familiar surroundings requires something akin to genius. To be sure, he was helped by all the books he could obtain, especially by Springer's *Forest Life and Forest Trees,* to which he was indebted for both matter and manner; from which he learned to narrow his field of observation to the woods and the Indian, leaving other topics of interest unexamined. But how did he know, unless he discerned it in Springer's account of them, that these remote woods farms, in his day (not now), were "winter quarters"? How did he understand (and this he surely did not get from Springer) that it is the moose, and not the bear nor the beaver, which is "primeval man"? How came he to perceive the Homeric quality of the men of the woods? Hardly would the chance tourist see so much. And he can explain the Homeric times by these: "I have no doubt that they lived pretty much the same sort of life in the Homeric age, for men have always thought more of eating than of fighting; then, as now, their minds ran chiefly on 'hot bread and sweet cakes;' and the fur and lumber trade is an old story to Asia and Europe." And, with a sudden illumination, "I doubt if men ever made a trade of heroism. In the days of Achilles, even, they delighted in big barns, and perchance in pressed hay, and he who possessed the most valuable team was the best fellow."

So, though he was neither woodsman nor scientist, Thoreau stood at the gateway of the woods and opened them to all future comers with the key of poetic insight. And after the woods shall have passed away, the vision of them as he saw them will remain. In all that was best in him Thoreau was a poet. The finest passages in this book are poetical, and he is continually striking out some glowing phrase, like a spark out of flint. The logs in the camp are "tuned to each other with the axe." "For beauty give me trees with the fur on." The pines are for the poet, "who loves them like his own shadow in the air." Of the fall of a tree in the forest, he says, "It was a dull, dry, rushing sound, with a solid core to it, like the shutting of a door in some distant entry of the damp and shaggy wilderness." Katahdin is "a permanent shadow." And upon it, "rocks, gray, silent rocks, were the silent flocks and herds that pastured, chewing a rocky cud at sunset. They looked at me with hard gray eyes, without a bleat or low." I have seen the rocks on many granite hills, but that belongs only to the top of Katahdin.

Indeed, this whole description of Katahdin is unequaled. "Chesuncook" is the best paper of the three, taken as a whole, but these few pages on Katahdin are incomparable. Happily he knew the traditions of the place, the awe and veneration with which the Indians regarded it as the dwelling-place of Pamola, their god of thunder, who was angry at any invasion of his home and resented it in fogs and sudden storms. ("He very angry when you gone up there; you heard him gone oo-oo-oo over top of gun-barrel," they used to say.) Thoreau's Katahdin was a realm of his own, in which for a few hours he lived in primeval solitude above the clouds, invading the throne of Pamola the Thunderer, as Prometheus harried Zeus of his lightnings. The gloomy grandeur of Æschylus rises before him to give him countenance, and he speaks himself as if he wore the buskin. But it is not windy declamation. He does not explode into exclamation points. Katahdin is a strange, lone, savage hill, unlike all others,—a very Indian among mountains. It does not need superlatives to set it off. Better by far is Thoreau's grim humor, his calling it a "cloud factory," where they made their bed "in the nest of a young whirlwind," and lined it with "feathers plucked from the live tree." Had he been one of the Stonish men, those giants with flinty eyebrows, fabled to dwell within the granite vitals of Katahdin, he could not have dealt more stout-heartedly by the home of the Thunder-God.

The best of Thoreau's utterances in this volume are like these, tuned to the rapid and high vibration of the poetic string, but not resolved into rhythm. It is poetry, but not verse. Thoreau's prose stands in a class by itself. There is an honest hardness about it. We may accept or deny Buffon's dictum that the style is the man; but the man of soft and slippery make-up would strive in vain to acquire the granitic integrity of structure which marks Thoreau's writing. It is not poetical prose in the ordinary scope of that flowery term; but, as the granite rock is rifted and threaded with veins of glistening quartz, this prose is fused at white heat with poetical insights and interpretations. Judged by ordinary standards, he was a poet who failed. He had no grace at metres; he had no æsthetic softness; his sense always overruled the sound of his stanzas. The fragments of verse which litter his workshop remind one of the chips of flint about an Indian encampment. They might have been the heads of arrows, flying high and singing in their flight, but that the stone was obdurate or the maker's hand was unequal to the shaping of it. But the waste is nothing; there is behind them the Kineo that they came from, this prose of his, a whole mountain of the same stuff every bit capable of being wrought to ideal uses.

[1917]

Perhaps the most penetrating essay that appeared to mark the centennial of Thoreau's birth in 1917 is one that lies almost completely forgotten in the pages of a short-lived little magazine, The Seven Arts. Although it was put out of circulation almost before it began, because of its pacifism in a world of war, it managed to print more thoughtful articles, more first-rate literature than almost any other magazine of its time.

HENRY DAVID THOREAU (1817-1917)

BY THE EDITORS OF The Seven Arts

It is a hundred years this month since Thoreau was born (July 12, 1817). Perfectly self-coherent as he was and, unlike most writers, the embodiment of all his ideas, he marks better perhaps than any other figure in our social history the distance we have travelled in our progress from the unity of the one to the unity of the many. "The universe," he said, "is always on the side of the most sensitive." The world, in the long run, is always on the side of those who have been able to contrive some definite pattern out of life. Thoreau's pattern was that of the pioneer mind itself, which in him realized its height and depth. Unwilling as he was to yield his allegiance to any ideas which the instincts of his fellow-countrymen had not entitled them to, he gave no hostages to the ever-shifting fabric of a society that had no fund of ideals verified in the general experience of the race. That is why he has outlasted so many of his more gifted contemporaries, lightly caught out of themselves, lightly undone. He knew how

From *Seven Arts,* II (July, 1917), 383-85.

primitive at bottom was the life that surrounded him, and like
Whitman the only men he really respected were men close to the
elements, the forest, the sea, the soil. It was among such alone
that he was able to discover the perfect integrity which he exacted
from living things and found in such abundance in trees and
animals. It was this that led him to look with the aloofness of an
immortal upon the world out of which he had grown like a resinous
and vibrant little hemlock, solitary and disdainful among the
ephemeridae of an April meadow. For Thoreau, whose imagination never compassed the gelatinous mass of humankind, society
meant nothing but the infringement of the individual. "Blessed
are the young," he said, "for they never read the President's
message." He was an anarchist not through the wisdom of the
serpent but the innocence of the dove, a skeptical innocence that
allowed nothing to pass without proof. Our original "man from
Missouri," he never forgot, however, that skepticism degrades
itself when it stands guard not over the ends but over the means
of life. So far as the means were concerned, it was impossible
for Thoreau to take them seriously at all; he was literally "out
from under" society by virtue of a continence like that of a lone
goldfish in a glass of ice-water. And he was as unsinkable as a
cork, thanks to the universal tinker's genius with which his nim-
blehanded forebears had endowed him. His disdainfulness, no
doubt, came a little cheap, and his immortal airs would not have
been less convincing had they been put to the test of mortal desire.
But then he would not have been the perfectly typical man he
was, he would not have been able to flatter us now with a sense
of our own immeasurable advance in frank self-knowledge and
free experience.

As it is, he flatters us quite enough. In much that our generation holds dear, Thoreau was poor indeed. His emotional rigidity,
for example, must have been unique even in Concord. A young
girl once complained that having taken her to the top of a mountain, he fixed his earnest gaze on a distant point in the landscape

and remarked, "How far is it in a bee-line to that spot?" It is conceivable, of course, that he had other thoughts then and on similar occasions, but they never found expression even in his verse. Practical enough to be able to regulate even the beating of his pulse, he kept the chambers of his mind in perfect order by packing everything that got in his way up into the attic of Transcendentalism. A capacious attic that was indeed, without which Concord could hardly have existed at all. It contained, among other things, a veritable Pandora's box full of all the amorous plagues that confuse and terrify mankind. But never a germ escaped. It had been locked for generations and the key had been hidden away, heaven knows where, in the old world, and the dust had gathered on it, and it had been forgotten. Yet how much they owed to that box, the philosophers of Concord! Never before or since have high thinkers and plain livers had smoother sailing.

With regard to the objective world, moreover, Thoreau leaves off where we begin. But might it not be added that we begin on the hither side of a great many important things the secret of which he possessed and we have lost? His imagination, unlike Emerson's absolutely concrete, required a commensurate field of fact of a sort that society only affords where a certain number of people have disengaged themselves from necessity and accepted parts in the tragi-comedy of the free life. Half a dozen of his contemporaries had taken this step: Thoreau made the most of them. John Brown, Whitman, and one or two others, as we know, appealed to him even more than bumblebees; but one swallow does not make a summer and a handful of individuals cannot make the corporate life significant if it has no significance without them. Besides, to the beasts of the field Thoreau could allow a certain latitude; precisely because, having no souls, they never whine about them, as Whitman said, they offered him an unlimited scope for a purely pagan delight. The sensuous and dramatic in man could not have passed the censorship of his multifarious principles; toward the rest of creation he could adopt without compunction the role of the free spectator, "clear of the nets of right and wrong."

I have said that he possessed a secret which we have lost. It was the secret of the sensuous life in a rich objective world. The life of nature meant more to Thoreau than the life of man has meant to any of our novelists, in its appeal, I mean, to the eye, the ear, the touch, the taste. There are pages in "Walden" which, by contrast, show up our American fiction, despite its occasional glamour, its frequent finesse, for the poor unpalatable straw it mostly is. To Thoreau there was a perceptible music in the universe, an Æolian music, and it was not through the contemplative inner ear that he received it, as Emerson did,—he heard it as plainly as a sensitive modern ear hears the music of humankind in the rhythm of city streets. It was this that gave him his marvellous power, like that of Saint Francis, over the lower orders, in which he divined an unconscious aspiration. The fox he characterized as "a rudimentary, burrowing man" and it disturbed him that we treat horses merely as automata to get work from, without any sense of responsibility to the spark of life that glimmers in them. It would be easier to find these complaints altogether absurd were they not bound up with a certain faculty possessed by Thoreau which testified to a profound grasp of the invisible forces. Rowing on Walden Pond, for example, he would put his hand into the water and gently lift out a fish which, after a moment's caress, would lie motionless across his palm for the space of half an hour. Feats like this gave him in the eyes of the village children a glamour like that which surrounded Virgil in the Middle Ages. The spiritual powers that made them possible, translated to the written page, constitute a lost province in our literary mind.

It is not this, however, it is not even his atavistic and half animal simplification of life, so alluring in certain ways just now, for which we remember him; it is the firmness of his personal texture, the force with which he enclosed and cultivated the little garden-plot of his own character. Stevenson called him a "skulker," Lowell said that his whole life was a search for the doctor. But there is something solid in Thoreau, beside which these two engaging literary entertainers of an optimistic and highly self-delusive past ring exceedingly hollow. He was as queer as Dick's hatband and he rubs most modern philosophy the wrong way. As for his prose, it contains passages of the kind which people used to call imperishable and which our contemporaries take a special delight in forgetting just for that reason. But in spite of everything he has never quite lost his tenacious grip on our imagination. Is it because of the conscientious objector in him, which our indeterminate and facile democracy has always found it so hard to forgive? At bottom we love self-discipline, we love obstacles, we love austerity, and Thoreau is a perpetual reminder, the most vivid reminder our history affords us, that it is the toughness, the intransigence of the spiritual unit which alone gives edge to democracy. As our epoch of expansion draws to its close and we are obliged more and more to test the mettle of our social consciousness, we shall be brought back to this truth, apprehended in so many ways by our fathers in the forest. The day will come when easy solutions no longer have any charm for us and we shall have attained the strength to fashion ourselves in the face of the multitudinous modern world. Then Thoreau will delight us anew, —not least because the gate of *his* Utopia was a needle's eye.

[1921]

Norman Foerster, another of the leaders of the Humanists, was one of the pioneers in introducing the study of American literature into the college curriculum. Primarily interested in the role of "nature in American literature," he wrote numerous essays on Thoreau. This study of Thoreau as a stylist is one of the few thoroughgoing essays in that field.

THOREAU AS ARTIST

BY NORMAN FOERSTER

I

Inveterate observer and recorder that he was, at heart Thoreau was assuredly not a naturalist, but rather—what? A literary artist? This answer, one of the commonest, has behind it not only the authority of his friend Channing, who said that Thoreau regarded literature as his profession, but also that of Thoreau himself, who declared, in unmistakable terms: "My work is writing." Yet it must be remembered that in his lifetime he published only two books, the *Week* and *Walden*; that the creative impulse in him was neither vehement nor persistent, most of his *Journal* being a bare record of facts; and that he wanted both the spur of fame and the desire to serve men, at least as these aims are usually conceived by writers. If writing was his work, it was his work in much the same sense in which surveying and pencil-making were his work: he was not a surveyor or manufacturer of pencils, nor was he a man of letters.

From *Sewanee Review*, XXIX (January, 1921), 2-13, by permission.

Poet, at all events, he was not, for a man can scarcely be a poet without achieving a certain bulk of successful verse, and the total bulk of Thoreau's verse, most of it unsuccessful, would fill less than an ordinary volume. That he wrote it at all is to be explained less in terms of his artistic powers, since he lived in a time of renaissance when the homespun of prose was disparaged in favor of purple singing-robes, in a time when, it has been said, one could not throw a stone in the city of Boston without hitting a poet. So Thoreau versified; his prose works abound in interjected poems or poetic fragments, many of which have the odd effect of serving, not to lift the reader aloft on the wings of sudden inspiration, but to make him halt in consternation before a veritable New England glacial boulder, shapeless and inert. There is little in him of the lyrical poet's instinct to burst into song at every provocation of nature. Although he tells us repeatedly that he is inspired, he also tells us that the mood is gone before he can versify it; the best poetry, he says broadly, is never expressed— an assertion not without its measure of truth. Indeed, it was fatally true of his own practice. Delicately perceptive of the concrete world, eagerly responsive to beauty, inwardly living the life of the poet, he was so intent on understanding and appropriating his visions that when the time came for singing them he was dumb.

THE POET'S DELAY

In vain I see the morning rise,
    In vain observe the western blaze,
Who idly look to other skies,
    Expecting life by other ways.

Shall I then wait the autumn wind,
    Compelled to seek a milder day,
And leave no curious nest behind,
    No woods still echoing to my lay?

In these lines is something of his Puritanical distrust of all art; "very dangerous", he says elsewhere, is the talent for composition, since "I feel as if my life had grown more outward when I can express it." With him it is always *my life,* never the glory of divine poetry:—

> "My life hath been the poem I would have writ,
> But I could not both live and live to utter it."

In natural metrical skill he was more deficient even than Emerson. Most of his verses are benumbed, and crawl along, with an occasional spurt, like a grasshopper in the autumn. For example:—

> "Let such pure hate still underprop
> Our love, that we may be
> Each other's conscience,
> And have our sympathy
> Mainly from thence."

If Donne deserved hanging for not keeping of accent, what of Thoreau? The following is a more just specimen, typical in subject, form, and mood:—

TALL AMBROSIA

> Among the signs of autumn I perceive
> The Roman wormwood (called of learned men
> *Ambrosia elatior,* food for gods,
> For by impartial science the humblest weed
> Is as well named as is the proudest flower)
> Sprinkles its yellow dust over my shoes
> As I brush through the now neglected garden.
> We trample under foot the food of gods
> And spill their nectar in each drop of dew.
> My honest shoes, fast friends that never stray
> Far from my couch, thus powdered, countrified,
> Bearing many a mile the marks of their adventure,
> At the post-house disgrace the Gallic gloss
> Of those well-dressed ones who no morning dew
> Nor Roman wormwood ever have done through,
> Who never walk, but are transported rather,
> For what old crime of theirs I do not gather.

In such lines he is a forerunner of Robert Frost; if Emerson's judgment is right, he could also be a successor and improver of

Simonides, as in the best of all his poems, the Walden verses on
"Smoke":—

> "Light-winged Smoke, Icarian bird,
> Melting thy pinions in thy upward flight;
> Lark 'without song, and messenger of dawn,
> Circling above the hamlets as thy nest;
> Or else, departing dream and shadowy form
> Of midnight vision, gathering up thy skirts;
> By night star-veiling, and by day
> Darkening the light and blotting out the sun; —
> Go thou, my incense, upward from this hearth,
> And ask the gods to pardon this clear flame."

Virtually blank verse, this delicate yet classically firm little poem
suggests the possibilities of that form for lyrical use. Had Thoreau
lived in the England of Elizabeth, he might well have been a
builder of lofty rhyme; like Whitman, although for other reasons,
he was a great poet *in posse*.

His poetic feeling, however, is worthily embalmed in his prose.
Moments of inspiration, as he remarks, are not lost merely because
they fail to leave a deposit in verse; the impression abides, and
in due time is expressed in a form equally genuine if less ardent:
when time has emphasized the essential truth in these ecstatic
states,—

"in cooler moments we can use them as paint to gild and adorn our
prose. . . . They are like a pot of pure ether. They lend the writer when
the moment comes a certain superfluity of wealth, making his expression to overrun and float itself."

Without this superfluity of wealth, Thoreau's prose would be shorn
of most of its beauty and power. If not a great poet, Thoreau is
a great prose writer.

II

The first and last impression produced by Thoreau's prose is
its sincerity, its unflinching truth. It is faithfully idiosyncratic, the
mirror of his sincerity of character. "I would rather sit on a

pumpkin and have it all to myself than be crowded on a velvet cushion"—who but Thoreau could have written that? Speaking of the art of writing, Thoreau leans upon that universally applicable maxim of the transcendentalists: "Be faithful to your genius!" This is for him the central precept.

"The one great rule of composition — and if I were a professor of rhetoric I should insist on this — is, to *speak the truth*. This first, this second, this third: pebbles in your mouth or not."

He was instinctively and somewhat bitterly suspicious of "the *belles-lettres* and the *beaux arts* and their *professors, which we can do without.*" He would simply say, with Buonaparte: "Speak plain; the rest will follow," with his eye on the truth and not on the ornaments. He would not seek expressions, but thoughts to be expressed—and even this did not satisfy him, for best of all, he says somewhere, is "the theme that seeks me, not I it". He is only to report, to obey, to serve as agent, to lend himself to an utterance "free and lawless as a lamb's bleat": an account true enough of his habit if one bears in mind that he was a somewhat wolfish lamb bred in a highly civilized tradition. His distinction in this matter, however, is not in his theory of style, which is the common property of the romantic school, but in his practice, which is all but unequalled in its resoluteness. Cardinal Newman, despite his admirable statement of the two-fold aspect of style, of the marriage of thought and word, and his assertion that his own aim was to express truth with no admixture of rhetoric, clearly enough was enamored of Roman eloquence. Similarly, to take an instance from Thoreau's Rome, the youthful Emerson, relishing resounding phrases and noble periods, never, in later years, quite freed himself from the seductions of adventitious beauty. The ideal of Emerson's style, says Mr. Brownell, is eloquence; that of Thoreau's, we may add in contrast, is truth. So rigorously does Thoreau follow his ideal that he demands of every sentence that it be "the result of a long probation", expressing in words what had already been expressed in action. He applies this ideal, not only to writing, but quite as much to reading. "What I began by reading," he says, "I must finish by acting." In a good book he looked first of all, perhaps, for the gadfly in it, and rejoiced in its sting, not unlike the Puritans of the old Concord who magnified their sins and lashed them with a grim joy. It may well be that the idiosyncratic quality of Thoreau's prose style springs more from the Puritan in him than from the romanticist, more from the voice of conscience than from the "lamb's bleat".

The charm of Thoreau's prose rests, then, on its complete sincerity, and his prose is to be enjoyed to the full only by readers who find his personality attractive. Yet it has definite qualities that win the approval of any discriminating reader. His sentences, for one thing, are alive. Living in his way, an intense life constantly alert to what was going on in his inner being and in nature, he could not well write a page devoid of life, like the flaccid writing of the ordinary journalist. A writer without a full experience, as he says, used "torpid words, wooden or lifeless words, such words as 'humanitary', which have a paralysis in their tails". His own diction is fresh, dewy, an early morning diction. It has the enormous advantage of unusual concreteness—to be expected of a writer whose perceptions were so highly trained, and whose aversion was metaphysics. And his store of concrete words and images he used with gusto, if not abandon, responding to his theme, seeking to penetrate, by sympathy, to its heart or essence, as in this perfect account of the nighthawk's antic swoop and boom:—

"The night-hawk circled overhead in the sunny afternoons — for I sometimes made a day of it — like a mote in the eye, or in heaven's eye, falling from time to time with a swoop and a sound as if the heavens were rent, torn at last to very rags and tatters, and yet a seamless cope remained."

That slight turn, "or in heaven's eye", with its unexpected shifting of the image, is typical of his restrained animation. Or take the following instance of his expressiveness, with its "puff-ball" figure drawn straight from nature, its fit phrasing, and its satiric *aplomb*:—

"On gala days the town fired its great guns, which echo like pop-guns in these woods, and some waifs of martial music occasionally penetrate thus far. To me, away there in my bean-field at the other end of the town, the big guns sounded as if a puff-ball had burst; and when there was a military turn-out of which I was ignorant, I have sometimes had a vague sense all the day of some sort of itching and disease in the horizon, as if some eruption would break out there soon. . . ."

Figures of speech abound in such passages, as in all his writing—his concreteness is largely a figurativeness. His acquaintance with nature is, of course, reflected in his metaphors and similes, as in that perfect comparison of the big guns with a puff-ball; or in his comparison of the weeping of Ossian's heroes with the perspiration of stone in the heat of summer; or in his comparison of the man of intellect with a barren, staminiferous flower, and of the poet with a fertile and perfect flower; or in that graphic comparison, mentioned by Channing, of the branches of Darby's oak with gray lightning stereotyped on the sky.

His love of paradox, his fondness for puns (in which he rivals his favorite poets of the great period of English literature), and the ever-present element of surprise in his style, are additional manifestations of his desire fully to rouse himself and his reader to the inner nature of his theme, whether it be night-hawks, or celebrations by the rude bridge that spanned the river, or the sense of time and space. A penetrating impression must be made, at all costs. He is never, or almost never, languid, but holds his stilus firmly, as in this sentence, which illustrates its own meaning:—

"A sentence should read as if the author, had he held a plow instead of a pen, could have drawn a furrow deep and straight to the end."

Here the emphasis falls distinctly and precisely where it should fall; so does it, to take another example, in this:—

"When the wind blows, the fine snow comes filtering down through all the aisles of the wood in a golden cloud."

A penetrating effect, again, is achieved by his conciseness. Writing of De Quincey, Thoreau remarks that a good style must have a strength in reserve, must be "concentrated and nutty". His own style, especially in the satiric and critical passages, is compact and germinal, acridly nutty, like an acorn:—

"Do not stay to be an overseer of the poor, but endeavor to become one of the worthies of the world."

"Time is but the stream I go a-fishing in."

"It takes a man to make a room silent."

"One man may well feel chagrined when he finds he can do nearly all he can conceive."

"How can we expect a harvest of thought who have not had a seed-time of character?"

He would not spread himself thin, either in his life or in his writing. Everything must be deliberate and concentrated.

"The writer must direct his sentences as carefully and leisurely as the marksman his rifle, who shoots sitting and with a rest, with patent sights and conical balls beside."

And indeed, as a stylist, Thoreau is something of a marksman; now his sentences crack close at hand, now they sound as from a remoter station, reverberating solemnly, as if nature had taken them unto herself and charged them with a meaning of her own.

Such command is invaluable in satire and wit. Humor, that "indispensable pledge of sanity", he had, but a good-natured spontaneous wit, with a trace of sharpness, was more characteristic. Says Channing:—

"There was a lurking humor in almost all that he said, — a dry wit, often expressed. He used to laugh heartily and many times in all the intercourse I had, when anything in that direction was needed. . . . No one more quickly entertained the apprehension of a jest; and his replies often came with a startling promptness."

Instances are everywhere, even in the sober *Journal,* as when he tells of a party, warm and noisy, where he suffered himself to be introduced to two young women, one of whom "was as lively and loquacious as a chickadee; had been accustomed to the society of watering-places, and therefore could get no refreshment out of such a dry fellow as I", while the other, said to be pretty, could not make herself heard, "there was such a clacking", and he sagely concludes that parties are social machinery designed for matrimonial connections, and prefers to eat crackers and cheese in the silent woods with old Joseph Hosmer. Or take the following reaction to the *ewig Weibliche*:—

"When you are once comfortably seated at a public meeting, there is something unmanly in the sitting on tiptoe and *qui vive* attitude, — involuntary rising into your throat, as if gravity had ceased to operate, — when a lady approaches, with quite godlike presumption, to elicit the miracle of a seat where none is."

Or finally this, in a milder vein, on a Puritan method of paying the clergy:—

" 'In 1662, the town agreed that a part of every whale cast on shore be appropriated for the support of the ministry.' No doubt there seemed to be some propriety in thus leaving the support of the ministers to Providence, whose servants they are, and who alone rules the storms; for, when few whales were cast up, they might suspect that their worship was not acceptable. The ministers must have sat upon the cliffs in every storm, and watched the shore with anxiety."

Much of the charm of Thoreau's best pages resides in this lurking humor, this dry wit always ready to kindle. Without them, he might have been an intolerably disagreeable social critic, though he might still have written pleasantly of nature,—a possibility not so remote when we learn that in his last years he blotted the humorous parts of his essays, saying: "I cannot bear the levity I find". He spoke like Endicott at Merry Mount.

III

With Carlyle and Ruskin and other typical writers of his century, Thoreau obviously excelled in the expressive side of art; but what of form? His sense of form has been placed with Emerson's (Emerson, to speak brusquely, having none). It is true that both Transcendentalists had the same weaknesses, even preparing their essays in the same manner by extorting them, so to say, out of their jewel-laden diaries. There is, however, a difference of degree. Thoreau's sentences and paragraphs cohere better than do Emerson's: he generally leaves the impression of continuity even when he lacks the reality, while Emerson often has the reality without leaving the impression. Thoreau, that is, writes from Parnassus, Emerson from Delphi. Thoreau again, if less noble, is more luminous—not only because his subjects are different, but also because his mode of thinking is more concrete. Although wanting a true sense of the value of architectonics in literature, he loved shapeliness, fine carving, beauty of form, "elegance", as he termed it—the informing quality that is simply the flowering of a nature well-tempered and wisely civilized, a humane nature. Much of this love of beauty he must have derived from his intimate studies in Greek and Latin literatures. "I do not know," he remarks, "but the reason why I love some Latin verses more than whole English poems is simply in the elegant terseness and conciseness of the language." His feeling for beauty is thus not unlike that of the school of Pope and Dr. Johnson, although in saying this one should remember that he all but ignored the eighteenth century and differed far from Johnson in regarding *Lycidas* as perhaps the finest example of true elegance in English. In his own work he attained in large measure his ideal of elegance, partly through revision (a facile writer, he resorted constantly to the use of the file), and partly through his realizing in his character something of the classical decorum. He believed that beauty is the final excellence, that whereas a first inspection of good writing should reveal its common-sense, a second should reveal its severe truth, and a third beauty.

He was well fitted to see beauty in external nature. Coming back to nature from the ancient classics, he perceived with added force the meaning of the third of "those celestial thrins",—Truth, Goodness, Beauty,—in the loveliness of line, and light and shade, and color. Despite his provincial ignorance of the plastic arts— an ignorance emulating Emerson's—he succeeded in some degree in acquiring the point of view of the plastic arts through training his eye for landscape. Again and again in his writings he dominates the natural scene, composing it with the craftman's sense of design, displaying a feeling for balance, repetition, emphasis, harmony, quite apart from his feeling for spiritual significance lurking behind or expressed by outer beauty. He could enjoy beauty as such. His layman's interest in aesthetic principles is indicated by his careful reading of William Gilpin on landscape, and of Ruskin's *Modern Painters*. When in the field he had a habit of now and then inclining his head to one side, or even stooping enough to reverse the picture completely in order to refresh himself with the ideal beauty suggested by the scene when thus severed from its normal associations. It is noteworthy that when the woodsmen come to desecrate his Walden pine groves he does not tremble to the foundations, but calmly remarks: "It makes some new and unexpected prospects", and while these prospects are in the making quietly enjoys the picture before him: "A pretty forest scene, seeing oxen, so patient and stationary, good for pictures, standing on the ice,—a piece of still life." One of the woodchoppers "appeared to me apparently half a mile distant, as in a picture of which the two trees were the frame". After an extended description of this picture, he observes that some scenes have an obvious pictorial quality, needing no composition, no idealization, being already pictures, ready for the recording pencil.

Such pictures he was constantly watching for, training himself to recognize them when others would have passed them by. He would be an artist as well as a naturalist. Daily, while living in town, he took occasion to view the sunset, that ever-repeated yet never-repeated masterpiece of nature: "Every day a new picture is painted and framed, held up for half an hour, in such lights as the Great Artist chooses, and then withdrawn." Everywhere he looked for new 'effects' wrought by that Artist, the master *improvvisatore,* in the flowing world of nature. He never tired of seeing the familiar meadows, woods, ponds, and hills of Concord varied without repetition by his shifting points of view and by the always unique caprices of the weather: he was as active in this aesthetic pursuit as in his scientific interest in names, dates, and temperatures. To-day he beholds Walden remote and eerie in the mist; to-morrow he shall thrill to the "clear, cold, Novemberish light" that glitters from downy twigs and lies vividly upon the "silver-plated river". He stands on Strawberry Hill late on a misty September afternoon: "Annursnack never looked so well as now seen from this hill. The ether gives a velvet softness to the whole landscape. The hills float in it. A blue veil is drawn over the earth." Thus day after day and year after year he studied the landscapes of Concord.

The result of all this study was the inimitable charm, the intimate mastery, of all of his descriptions of nature, whether an individual leaf or the whole of a vast prospect. That sensuous equipment that served him as an observer of natural fact, served him equally as an observer of natural beauty, giving him a high degree of truth in both spheres. What other writer of our time has perceived so subtly and expressed his vision with so delicate a truth? Ruskin, beside Thoreau, seems theatrical, melodramatic, entranced by his own powers, giving nature the stamp of his expansive personality: Thoreau's self-restraint steadies his insight, lets him penetrate closer to the heart of nature as to his own heart. His magical truth has won him many a devoted reader who finds himself indifferent to, or exasperated by, Thoreau's personal piquancy and his paradoxical satire of human society. Who that knows *Walden* can forget those glorious white pines of "Baker Farm"?—   .

"Sometimes I ramble to pine groves, standing like temples, or like fleets at sea, full-rigged, with wavy boughs, and rippling with light, so soft and green and shady that the Druids would have forsaken their oaks to worship in them."

One sentence could scarcely do more. Or take his reproduction of the song of the red-winged blackbird, whose liquid notes fill the meadows in early spring:—

"The strain of the red-wing on the willow spray over the water to-night is liquid, bubbling, watery, almost like a twinkling fountain, in perfect harmony with the meadow. It oozes, trickles, tinkles, bubbles from its throat, — *bob-y-lee-e-e,* and then its shrill, fine whistle."

Or take his exquisite insight into the beauty of the leaves of the tree known as the scarlet oak:—

"Stand under this tree and see how finely its leaves are cut against the sky, — as it were, only a few sharp points extending from a midrib. They look like double, treble, or quadruple crosses. They are far more ethereal than the less deeply scalloped oak leaves. They have so little leafy *terra firma* that they appear melting away in the light, and scarcely obstruct our view. . . . Lifted higher and higher, and sublimated more and more, putting off some earthiness and cultivating more intimacy with the light each year, they have at length the least possible amount of earthy matter, and the greatest spread and grasp of skyey influences. There they dance, arm in arm with the light, — tripping it on fantastic points, fit partners in those aerial halls. So intimately mingled with it are they, that, what with their slenderness and their glossy surfaces, you can hardly tell at last what in the dance is leaf and what is light. And when no zephyr stirs, they are at most but a rich tracery to the forest windows."

Or, once more, the beauty of Concord apples:—

". . . unspeakably fair, — apples not of Discord, but of Concord!
. . . Painted by the frosts, some a uniform clear bright yellow, or red, or crimson, as if their spheres had regularly revolved, and enjoyed the influence of the sun on all sides alike, — some with the faintest pink blush imaginable, — some brindled with deep red streaks like a cow, or with hundreds of fine blood-red rays running regularly from the stem-dimple to the blossom end, like meridional lines, on a straw-colored ground, — some touched with a greenish rust, like a fine lichen, here and there, with crimson blotches or eyes more or less confluent and fiery when wet, — and others gnarly, and freckled or peppered all over on the stem side with fine crimson spots on a white ground, as if accidentally sprinkled from the brush of Him who paints the autumn leaves. Others, again, are sometimes red inside, perfused with a beautiful blush, fairy food, too beautiful to eat, — apple of the Hesperides, apple of the evening sky!"

[1926]

*H. M. Tomlinson, considered by many one of the foremost prose
stylists today, has frequently acknowledged his debt to Thoreau.*

THOREAU

BY H. M. TOMLINSON

My two friends from New York looked out to the Thames from
an upper window of the Savoy Hotel. . . . The three of us began
to discuss English and American writers. We were painfully polite
to one another. We made free concessions of our pawns, as it
were, as though we did not wish to win the game. My friends
submitted, and I freely confessed, the vitality and significance of
the literary impulses in contemporary America. No doubt about
that vitality. But they regretted that America could not match the
old country yet with any star of the first magnitude—no Shelley,
no "Ode to the Nightingale," no "Christabel," no *Pickwick Papers;*
nothing of that size.

Heavens, I said to myself, what do these men want! What would
they call a big star? My mind fumbled backwards to the 'fifties
when, within a few years of one another, there appeared in the
United States *Leaves of Grass, Walden,* and *Moby Dick.* Enough
to satisfy any quiet community for a century! I glanced at my
friends, thought I could see how it was, and therefore made
bread pills, silently and respectfully. Evidently I was faced at this
luncheon with a very fine exhibit of transatlantic modesty. They
did not want me to feel sorry because England had nothing to

From "Two Americans and a Whale," *Harper's Magazine,* CLII (April, 1926),
618-21, by permission. Introductory remarks and the portions of the essay devoted
to Whitman and Melville have been deleted.

show of quite the stamp of those three works. I was forced at last to congratulate my friends on their noble sacrifice of an impregnable position. No doubt could remain any longer of the friendship of the two Anglo-Saxon peoples. "If an Englishman," I assured them, "had told the story of the White Whale we should not pretend that we thought it of no more than the usual significance, not for all the Americans in America. And we could not have grown *Leaves of Grass* at all. Victorian England was simply incapable of it."

Now there was no doubt of it. Another look at the two of them was enough to show that they were sorry to see me quite so embarrassingly polite. I mean, they did not believe me. Perhaps they even supposed that I was superiorly and ironically English. "Many Americans, perhaps most Americans," said one of them with great courtesy, "would hardly know what you meant if you spoke of *Walden* without sufficient references. I never knew that *Walden* counted for anything in England."

That left me helpless. When there is much to explain about a difficult matter, and you find unexpectedly that your audience is without the initial clues, where are you to begin? I have always regarded Thoreau as an original writer who would have worked changes in the body of any literature, however old its tradition. It was an early reading of Stevenson's essay on Thoreau which disclosed to me not Thoreau's deficiencies but Stevenson's own. I suppose Thoreau has done as much as any other writer to give my mind a cast, for I knew his principal works when I was young. He with his metaphysics did something to ruin a career which might have been luckier with more judicious guidance. There have been reviewers who have hinted at origins for my books, but not one of them has ever noticed that I must have brooded long on Walden Pond, in apparition, as a youth. I well remember my schoolmaster rebuking me for frequenting "that moonshine." Moonshine! But it was true; and we all know what strong moonlight is said to do for the careless head.

Though that, perhaps, is irrelevant. What Thoreau did for me is not evidence. But the knowledge of it, which I kept to myself, led me to tell the New Yorkers this story. More than thirty years ago there appeared in England a little book of which two million copies were sold. It was called *Merrie England*. It was a cogent and ruthless argument in political economy, written in a way which made that mystery plain to the simple man by his own fireside. That book, which sold in such numbers, which was used as a textbook by ardent reformers (nearly all of them young) in every market place and at almost every street corner in Great Britain, speeded perceptibly the popular impulse which has resulted in a first British Labor Government. Carlyle, Ruskin, and William Morris must not be forgotten. But they were then not greatly read by miners and such. It was *Merrie England* which woke them up. And Robert Blatchford, who wrote that forgotten book, betrays everywhere his debt to Whitman and Thoreau. Most of those ardent young disciples of Blatchford's carried *Walden* about with them. They founded literary societies in English industrial districts and named them after a little pond lost somewhere in New England, U.S.A. They could chant from *Leaves of Grass* as though it were a hymnal. Beware of young men when they turn to the poets and seers! People laugh to-day at the idea of faith removing mountains and point out that it took more than faith to cut the Panama Canal. But did it? They don't know what they are talking about. A few words will move the earth, if you give them time. . . .

I would not argue that Thoreau's philosophy, derived from the Orient (like all the great religions of the world), is any sort of a substitute for the famous *Manifesto* of Marx and Engels. The effect of his work was different from that of the *Manifesto,* of which most Englishmen, by the way, even if they vote Labor, know nothing but the last lines. But to those who have accepted, quite naturally, that purposeful and combative aspect of life which to our political economists is the only one in view, Thoreau seems as odd as would a Buddhist eremite to a stock-jobber. Yet a second and a steadier look at him may be disastrous to the Western concept of the strenuous life. You suspect, in sudden alarm, that there is more in life than you had been told; that it may have a nature hitherto unguessed, possibilities unknown; that, in fact, Western civilization may have taken the wrong path and may yet have to turn back—or wish desperately that it could. Marx does not do that. Thoreau's words, like those of another and far greater Teacher of an Oriental philosophy, simply dismiss with a little gesture most of our highly important activities, as a man might wave at an annoying fly. It would be ridiculous to suppose that the young men who once with enthusiasm, read *Walden* and "The Duty of Civil Disobedience" were any the more aware of the profound implications of those writings than are most convinced Christians of the Gospels. Still, give these things time. They work, they work. "The light that puts out our eyes is darkness to us. Only that day dawns to which we are awake. There is more day to dawn. The sun is but a morning star." . . .

[1929]

Thoreau has the ability to rub some people the wrong way. One could easily compile a Schimpflexikon *of Thoreauviana, just as H. L. Mencken did for his own critics. Unquestionably there is much to be said on the negative side — and it has been said with violence and abandon. Mr. Powys' essay is a keen and thoughtful denunciation.*

THOREAU: A DISPARAGEMENT

BY LLEWELYN POWYS

To a student of literature, it is interesting to observe how easily, I had almost said how fortuitously, certain men of letters have won that relative immortality which belongs to the craft of writing. In our eagerness to find some criterion, some absolute standard of worth in this difficult trade, we console ourselves with talk about the judgment of posterity, about the continual punctilious process of acceptance and rejection that is undertaken in each succeeding age "by the best minds" and which represents, so we assume, a deep instinct in the human race to preserve that which is of greatest value. There is more in this, however, than meets the eye. As in all human transactions, it is clear that chance or lucky accident plays a large part.

A good case in point is the work of Thoreau which I suspect has been and is today much overrated. Thoreau is cried up as being one of the greatest American writers. In reality, he was an awkward, nervous, self-conscious New Englander who, together with an authentic taste for oriental and classical literature, devel-

From the *Bookman* (New York), LXIX (April 1, 1929), 163-65, by permission.

oped a singular liking for his own home woods. He does not strike me as an original thinker, bolstered up as his thoughts always are by the wisdom of the past. Mysticism, that obstinately recurring form of human self-deception, is, in his case, even more unsatisfactory than usual, while his descriptions of nature that have won such applause are seldom out of the ordinary. I am inclined to think that his reputation owes much to his close association with Emerson, that truly great man, who under so kindly and sedate an exterior possessed so mighty a spirit.

The naivete of Thoreau's mind is incredible. At his best, he is second best. He is too cultured and not cultured enough. It is, in truth, amazing that this provincial pedant, who so strained to be original, should enjoy the distinction he does. "He was as local as a woodchuck," wrote John Burroughs. He observed nature closely but his most original passages are forced. His is a notebook observation, a very different thing from that deep underswell of passionate feeling that distinguishes, for example, the poetry of Walt Whitman when he chants of wild and free life. As I read this dilettante of the bluebird and the bobolink, I constantly find myself becoming impatient. He is too bookish, too literary. To draw direct power out of the ground, out of the smelling, fecund, sweet soil of the earth, it is necessary to lose oneself, it is necessary to lose one's soul to find it. Thoreau never is able to do this. He is always there, the transcendental original of Concord with a lesson to impart. It is impossible for him to feel nature in his lungs, in his navel, in the marrow of his bones. He must always have his journal-book within reach and must be fussing to enter on its pages some apothegm or apt description which he knows will later be commended by Emerson or by his less discerning lyceum audiences.

Thoreau plays at loving nature but his authentic background is not really in the cold woods as, for example, was the background of Thomas Bewick or even John Burroughs. We learn that he was extremely deft at making lead pencils. Emerson, always eager to praise his friend, testifies to this: "He could make as good a lead pencil as the English ones". Thoreau certainly used these dainty productions to some purpose, for what a murmur he made about his retreat at Walden Pond!

When we look into the matter there was really little enough "to it". At best, it was but a dramatic gesture. The celebrated hut was actually situated on the outskirts of Concord, within a mile and a half of the village, built on Emerson's land—in Emerson's yard, one might almost say. With an axe borrowed from his friend Alcott he constructed his habitation out of boards which had been conveyed to the woods from an Irishman's shanty. It was within sight of the railway and so close to the public highway that the woodland air was continually being impregnated with tobacco smoke from the pipes of wayfarers on the near-by road. Thoreau declares that he "never found the companion that was so companionable as solitude" but actually his house was constantly visited by friends. Indeed, it was fitted with a guest chamber. The undertaking was a form of pedantic play. The hermit himself often spent an evening in the village, returning in the dark, which was to him a great matter. "It is darker in the woods, even on common nights than most suppose." Bookworm that he was, the simplest country occupation fills him with self-conscious satisfaction. He records with pride how he came over the ice "trailing a dead pine tree under each arm to my shed". So little was he acquainted with the lore of the forest that he actually, on one occasion, when he was frying fish during one of his picnics, started a bush-fire which endangered the whole village of Concord!

Much of his writing is sheer affectation. He was asked whether he was not lonely and answered, "no more lonely than the loon on the pond that laughs so loud, or the Walden Pond itself. What company has that lovely lake, I pray. And yet it has not the blue devils, but the blue angels in it, in the azure tint of its waters". He goes for an excursion into Canada. "We styled ourselves Knights of the Umbrella and the Bundle". He was, in truth, a woodsman of the umbrella!

He is never weary of girding at the rich and conventional. "Simplicity, simplicity, simplicity," he exhorts and, then, the next moment can pen a sentence that has upon it the very stamp of finical banality. "The luxuriously rich are not simply kept comfortably warm but unnaturally hot; as I implied before, they are cooked, of course, *a la mode*." Sometimes it is as though he has no conception of what dignity of style means. He will call himself "the self-appointed inspector of snow-storms and rain-storms". "Our whole life is startlingly moral," he writes. "There is never an instant's truce between virtue and vice. Goodness is the only investment that never fails. In the music of the harp which trembles round the world it is the insisting on this which thrills us. The harp is the travelling patterer for the Universe's Insurance Company, recommending its laws, and our little goodness is all the assessment that we pay."

Perhaps it was the unfortunate upshot of his romantic attachment for Miss Ellen Sewall which gave his mind a cramped and crooked turn with regard to that emotion "before which all creation trembles and faints." The girl records that her father "wished me to write immediately in a short explicit and cold manner to Mr. Thoreau" and one wonders if the discouragement of the receipt of this letter did not help to dry up his already somewhat sapless nature. As the years passed Thoreau felt estranged from his indulgent patron, Emerson, and yet how he could have been instructed by that great man!

Give all to love;
Obey thy heart;

This back-door hermit has in his mouth all those convenient utterances that are in their very essence contrary to nature. He should have given more attention to the song of the hermit thrush! "Chastity is the flowering of man." "Man flows at once to God when the channel of purity is open." "He is blessed who is assured that the animal is dying out in him day by day, and the divine being established." Could he not have learned better doctrine from his Brooklyn friend, "the greatest democrat the world has ever seen"? We remember his utterance, "The soul is not greater than the body and the body is not greater than the soul". There is no end to Thoreau's Sunday School talk, "If you would avoid uncleanness, and all the sins, work earnestly though it be at cleaning a stable. Nature is hard to be overcome, but she must be overcome". We know now why we hear so much about his brave bean field on that lot of Emerson's which was in the opinion of a local farmer "good for nothing but to raise cheeping squirrels on".

And yet one must not be too captious. One must not depreciate unfairly this bookish philosopher. He does offer a charming picture of himself hoeing his beans, walking with bare feet from end to end of the lines while "green berries deepened their tints by the time I had made another bout". Yes, he is often able by some literary turn to give a freshness to his writing, this man who was "no more lonely than a single mullein or dandelion in a pasture . . . or the first spider in a new house". It is pleasant to think of him walking to Nine-Acre-Corner, or getting his feet wet in Becky Stow's swamp, or exploring some new "all-across-lot route," or gravely meditating how, with thrift, he could support life by using as his habitation "a large box in the railroad six feet long by three wide in which the laborers locked up their tools at night" while earning his daily bread by picking huckleberries.

It is possible from his pages to cull certain passages of wisdom. "This life is a strange dream and I don't believe at all any account men give of it." "There is no more fatal blunderer than he who consumes the greater part of his life getting his living." "The greater part of what my neighbors call good I believe in my soul to be bad, and if I repent of anything it is very likely to be my good behavior." "I wanted to live deep and suck out all the marrow of life." He can also give us glimpses of his life in the woods that have a true beauty, as, for example, when paddling about Walden Pond after dark he would see "perch and shiners, dimpling the surface with their tails in the moonlight". To those of us who love the American countryside, there is a magic in the mere enumeration of the familiar flora, the goldenrod, the St. John's wort, the sumach! And yet, even here, one can be jarred by his method of expression. In his journal we come upon this passage about skunk cabbages. And how discouraging its jocular tone seems when one remembers the sturdy growth of this swamp vegetation which heralds the coming of the spring by thrusting up through the chilled ground mottled, red, curling horns that smell of the arm pits of Pan! "If you are afflicted with melancholy at this season, go to the swamp and see the brave spears of skunk-cabbage buds already advanced toward a new year. Their grave-stones are not bespoken yet. Who shall be sexton to them? Is it the winter of their discontent? Do they seem to have lain down to die, despairing of skunk-cabbagedom? 'Up and at 'em' . . . 'Excelsior' . . . these are their mottoes."

Thoreau was a great reader of books of the ancient tradition, but he was neither a profound thinker nor a great writer, and that is the truth.

[1930]

*Surprisingly, no one has ever made a thoroughgoing study of
the influence of Thoreau's essay on "Civil Disobedience." It has
been the handbook of radical groups the world over for many,
many years. The anti-Nazi resistance movement in Continental
Europe used it effectively as a manual of arms during World War
II. And of course its most famous proponent was Mahatma
Gandhi, who always carried a copy of the essay with him whether
he was imprisoned or free. Henry Salt was the British biographer
of Thoreau.*

GANDHI AND THOREAU

BY HENRY S. SALT

The doctrine of Civil Disobedience, in view of the manner in
which it is being applied by Mr. Gandhi, cannot be said to be
in very good favour at the present time; nevertheless, it may be
worth while to recall the fact that it is not the East only that is
responsible for so unsettling a maxim, but that the West must
equally bear its portion of the guilt, inasmuch as Gandhi had a
distinguished predecessor in Thoreau.

It was as a protest against the United States war with Mexico,
and the sanction then given to negro slavery, that Thoreau, in
1845, found himself in antagonism to the State, and, refusing to
pay his taxes, was arrested and thrown into prison. "Henry, why
are you here?" was the question put to him by Emerson; and his
characteristic answer was, "Why are you *not* here?" The incident
ended, tamely enough, in the tax being paid by Thoreau's rela-

From the *Nation & Athenaeum*, XLVI (March 1, 1930), 728.

tives; but his essay on "Civil Disobedience," written two or three years later, is a forcible statement of the conditions under which, as it seemed to the writer, a man is justified in rebellion without violence.

Possibly it has occurred to some readers of Thoreau to wonder whether Gandhi, of whose civil disobedience we have for a long time heard so much, had read that essay; and it was at the suggestion of an American friend that, presuming on a slight acquaintance with him through our practice of vegetarianism, I ventured to write and ask him the question. His answer (I quote from a letter dated October 12th, 1929) was as follows:—

"My first introduction to Thoreau's writings was, I think, in 1907, or later, when I was in the thick of the passive resistance struggle. A friend sent me the essay on 'Civil Disobedience.' It left a deep impression upon me. I translated a portion for the readers of 'Indian Opinion in South Africa,' which I was then editing, and I made copious extracts for the English part of that paper. The essay seemed to be so convincing and truthful that I felt the need of knowing more of Thoreau, and I came across your Life of him, his 'Walden,' and other shorter essays, all of which I read with great pleasure and equal profit."

So it would seem that if there is trouble in India, over the practice of Civil Disobedience, Thoreau must be credited with his share of the blame, or of the praise, according to the point of view from which the question is regarded.

[1937]

Our first American Nobel Prize winner in literature was usually considered skeptical of the values of the American worthies. But Thoreau not only escaped his criticism; he drew his praise. Lewis often went out of his way to express his admiration of the Concordian, as in this brief essay which was ostensibly a review of Henry Seidel Canby's omnibus edition of Thoreau's works.

ONE MAN REVOLUTION

BY SINCLAIR LEWIS

Once upon a time in America there was a scholar who conducted a one-man revolution and won it. He died 75 years ago, and we aren't within 75 years of catching up with him. He was Henry Thoreau, who helped to make Concord, Mass., as vast as London. He wanted, more than anything else, to buy his own time, and not to "buy time" on the radio—that cosmic feat—but to buy it from life; and out of that time he wanted leisure, not to sleep or shout or show off to the neighbors, but to enjoy the fruits of his growing brains and the delights of his ever-sharpening eyes, that took in not the clumsy hewings of the Acropolis or the Taj Mahal, but the divine delicacies of twigs and bird wings and morning ripples on Walden Pond.

He did not merely want it. He did it. Devoting a shrewd Yankee brain to the accurate measuring of his own wants, he saw just how few things he needed to wear and eat and own in order to be comfortable. No half-jeering questions of his neighbors could induce him to toil—as surveyor, as pencil maker—for one pennyworth more. He built his own warm shack, and in it he lived

From *Newsweek*, X (November 22, 1937), 33.

with a dignity vaster than any harassed emperor. He was popular in his social set, though it was not composed of the humble Bedauxes of his day, but of swallows and chipmunks and sunfish, and other swift, elegant, and shining notabilities.

All this, with gaiety and warmth, he wrote out in "Walden," one of the three or four unquestionable classics of American literature; published in 1854 and more modern than Dos Passos. The greater noises of his human circle, such as Emerson and Hawthorne and Louisa May Alcott's powerfully argumentative papa, considered him amiable but idiotic, and he is outlasting all of them.

His Walden, and all that is important from his other books, with notes and biography by Henry S. Canby, in an 848-page volume handsomely published by Houghton Mifflin at $5, is the book-buy of the year. I am burning a candle in the hope that 100,000 copies will be given as Christmas presents this year, to all young persons who are, and very reasonably, worrying about their economic futures, all married couples envious of their friends' automobiles, all Communists, all reactionaries, and all who have been affected by a phenomenon which, if I remember, I mentioned last week, *i. e.,* Dale Carnegie, the Bard of Babbittry.

Regarding the enthusiastic doctrines of Dr. Carnegie, Thoreau wrote, 82 years before "How To" was published:

"It is very evident what mean and sneaking lives many of you live . . . lying, flattering, contracting yourselves into a nutshell of civility or dilating into an atmosphere of thin and vaporous generosity, that you may persuade your neighbor to let you make his shoes or his hat . . . making yourselves sick, that you may lay up something against a sick day . . . I have traveled a great deal in Concord; and everywhere, in shops, and offices, and fields, the inhabitants have appeared to me to be doing penance in a thousand remarkable ways."

I would not set Andrew Carnegie and Heywood Broun as the captains of our freedom, now that it is menaced by Italy, by Germany, by Japan—and by the United States of America. But Henry Thoreau I would set, and this man, to whom the very notion of dictatorship would be inconceivable, I would make the supreme Duce.

[1944]

When Carl Bode's edition of the Collected Poems of Henry Thoreau *appeared in 1943, scholars were given their first opportunity to examine Thoreau as a verse writer. The most thorough evaluation that appeared was this by Professor Wells of Columbia University.*

AN EVALUATION OF THOREAU'S POETRY

BY HENRY W. WELLS

Eighty-one years after the death of Henry Thoreau has appeared under the careful editorship of Carl Bode the first edition of Thoreau's verse to provide an adequate view of his poetical attainments. The story is, to say the least, unusual. One recalls that eighty years is more than twice the time required to give due appreciation to the lyric art of Emily Dickinson. At last we are able to arrive at a critical estimate of Thoreau's place in American poetry and to speculate upon how much influence his poems, now that they are fairly available, may exercise.

The long period of tepid praise or total silence has been occasioned not only by inadequate publicity but by inadequate criticism and understanding. He himself gradually yielded to the pressure of circumstances and, as years advanced, largely deserted verse for prose. His poems were commonly accused of rawness and lack of poetical refinement. Whatever their faults, they were not vulgar. The middle-class emotionalism and false optimism, monotonous rhythms and facile sentiments, found no place in his personally sincere, highly imaginative, and deeply expressive

From *American Literature*, XVI (May, 1944), 99-109.

lines. His poetic prose the public accepted, but found his verse prosaic. It possessed sterner qualities discoverable only in the most vigorous schools of poetry and foreign not only to the effeminate phase of nineteenth-century taste but to the true comprehension of other leaders of American thought, such as Emerson and Lowell.

When a poet views his own lyrics casually, however carefully he may have produced them, sends few of them to his friends and to but one or two periodicals, and publishes them for the most part as appendages to his prose, his readers can scarcely be expected to weigh their intrinsic value as literature. Moreover, when such poems do at last see print in a becoming form, they will at first almost inevitably be regarded a bit cavalierly. Even the editor in his Introduction scarcely ventures to check a natural impression that they were casual jottings left half finished or in a shape unsatisfying to their author and blithely discarded by him when he reached full maturity of authorship. This view is unhappily furthered by a wholly legitimate inclusion in the collected edition of some fifty or more items of a few lines each which are in truth trifles, abruptly broken off, lacking in their opening lines, or left palpably unrevised. To the enthusiast they may appear precious fragments but to the larger public they may well be the rotten apples which tend to spoil the entire barrel. They tempt us to miss the main point, which is that three quarters of the poems and some nine tenths of the total number of lines are of finished workmanship, so far, at least, as the author's taste and judgment admitted. No part of Thoreau's voluminous manuscripts shows such painstaking revision as his verse.

Almost all Thoreau's poetry may be regarded as the achievement of a conspicuously independent young man who resolutely declined to ape the popular fashions of his age. While Emily Dickinson quietly discarded much of the specious writing of her times and country, Thoreau displayed a more vigorous opposition. To a remarkable degree he turned away from the main streams of contemporary taste in poetry as directed by Wordsworth, Byron, and the younger British writers of his own day. To be sure, he loved Wordsworth, and his poetry betrays this love; but in its rugged, terse, and abrupt expression it shows an art fundamentally unlike Wordsworth's. Scarcely a single poem from his hand can be associated with American fashions soon to be securely established by Longfellow, Whittier, and Lowell. In short, he is unregenerately unorthodox so far as midnineteenth-century America is concerned. It is well known that his reading was very little in his contemporary fellow countrymen and widely disseminated among the English classics and the literatures of the world. His unusual grasp of Greek and Latin poetry and his exercises in the translation of classical verse, notably Pindar, at least indicate his scope. It is true that whatever he writes springs from his heart— the clearest evidence of his genuine poetic faculty. Yet one of the outstanding features of his work is this evidence of the fruits of his reading and prophetic insight. Of his major poems not a single specimen adheres narrowly to the norm of romantic verse at the time of its composition, although, as we shall see, some extraordinary variations on romantic themes are to be found. The American environment itself is clearly indicated by his art in only half a dozen pieces, which at least resemble though they do not entirely agree with Emerson's rugged, didactic manner. At least an equal number strongly suggest Horace and the pure classical vein itself. A few stand in a surprising relation to medieval thought, feeling, or verse patterns. Slightly more are in much the same style as the manly verse of the founder of British neo-classicism, Ben Jonson. The more mannered and pseudo-heroic eloquence of the English Augustans, as in James Thomson, is occasionally turned by Thoreau to his own purpose. A larger group of lyrics share the spiritual inwardness, lively imagination, and chaste exterior of the English seventeenth-century meta-physical poets, whom Thoreau read and grasped uncommonly well. The nervous vigor and high excitement of some of the spiritual or didactic poetry of the Revolutionary period, notably William Blake's, has striking analogues in the New England radical. Where his nature poetry and his expressions of exaggerated idealism, optimism, and enthusiasm most approximate the high romantic style, he still shows his characteristic independence in thought and feeling. Finally, the largest group of his most memorable poems, nearly a third of them, belongs when historically considered not so much with the past as with the future. Thoreau, like Emily Dickinson or Baudelaire, anticipates the bold symbolism, airy impressionism, stringent realism, and restless inconsistencies of twentieth-century poetry. In the art of poetry no less than in his metaphysics, the recluse of Walden made the world and its epochs his province.

> If with fancy unfurled
> You leave your abode,
> You may go round the world
> By the Old Marlborough Road.

Moreover, he is a spiritual cosmopolitan by virtue of his intuitive grasp of the poetic imagination of other periods than his own and not by any mere wealth of allusions which he plunders from abroad. None of Poe's exotic bric-a-brac glitters from his pages. He makes no display of his internationalism, for it is the most natural and instinctive thing about him. His allusions and images are drawn from common nature and from life as seen in the neighborhood of Concord. It is with the eye of the soul and not of the body that his art looks toward past, future, and the ultra-montane world.

His classical studies left him, while still in his teens, with a sense of form sufficiently rare in the comparatively formless nineteenth century. His insight is suggested by a few quatrains with a shapeliness resembling the Greek Anthology. In speaking of Thoreau's epigrams Emerson not unnaturally referred to Simonides. A less derivative and more creative poet than Landor, Thoreau transports the classical form to the New England scene; the form is revitalized, the scene reinterpreted:

> Not unconcerned Wachusett rears his head
> Above the field, so late from nature won,
> With patient brow reserved, as one who read
> New annals in the history of man.

The long and impressive ode entitled "Let such pure hate still underprop" is clearly fashioned with the strict Horatian sense of proportion. One of his more romantic nature poems ends with an obvious recollection of Horace; the bare New England trees are pictured thus:

> Poor knights they are which bravely wait
> The charge of Winter's cavalry,
> Keeping a simple Roman state,
> Disencumbered of their Persian luxury.

It is worth notice that he refers to several of his poems as odes. Moreover, his lyrics are often classical in content as well as in form. He appropriately expresses Platonic doctrine in a poem of strict classical outline, "Rumors from an Aeolian Harp." Much of the classical morality of life appealed to him, especially in his later years when the extremes of his naturalistic romanticism wore thin. In "Manhood" he sees man and not nature as master of human fate. Man guides nature to do his will, as he might guide a horse. Experience teaches him a doctrine of ripe humanism:

> And it doth more assert man's eminence
> Above the happy level of the brute
> And more doth advertise me of the heights
> To which no natural path doth ever lead,
> No natural light can ever light our steps,
> But the far-piercing ray that shines
> From the recesses of a brave man's eye.

Traces of thought and art more or less deliberately derived from medieval sources may at first seem incongruous in a lover of the Maine woods, but they are present in no negligible degree. Thus a surprising poem entitled "The Virgin" reveals her place in the Catholic system midway between Heaven and Earth, the Old Law and the New. This paradoxical account of Mary resembles her praise as put into the mouth of Saint Bernard by Dante, yet Thoreau follows the spirit rather than the letter of medieval sources:

With her calm, aspiring eyes
She doth tempt the earth to rise,
With humility over all,
She doth tempt the sky to fall.

In her place she still doth stand
A pattern unto the firm land
While revolving spheres come round
To embrace her stable ground.

If this poem does not consciously refer to the Virgin Mary, it affords at least a remarkable coincidence. Much more usual in his poetry than theological reminiscences are inheritances, conscious or unconscious, from medieval verse patterns, possibly with aid from the German lyric tradition. Thoreau is a keen metrical experimenter, seeking exotic devices, both in rhyme and a free blank verse, to express his highly various moods. He revives Skeltonic measures, dimeter in general, and a dipodic verse typical of medieval poetry no less than of nursery rhymes. Metrically, and to some degree verbally, such a stanza as the following carries us back to the inspired doggerel of medieval mystery plays:

The axe resounds,
And bay of hounds
And tinkling sounds
Of wintry fame;
The hunter's horn
Awakes the dawn
On field forlorn,
And frights the game.

But to Thoreau the poetry and culture of the Middle Ages must indeed have seemed an interlude. To his ear as an English-speaking poet the classical manner which he loved was to be heard most forcibly rendered in English by Ben Jonson, father of English neoclassicism, and by Jonson's most intimate followers. Their simple and disciplined style leaves an unmistakable mark upon the wholly unaffected elegy, "Brother Where Dost Thou Dwell." The balanced and severely controlled style is crystallized in "Inspiration":

> I hearing get who had but ears,
> And sight, who had but eyes before,
> I moments live who lived but years,
> And truth discern who knew but learning's lore.

Also from the English seventeenth century Thoreau drew a poetic heritage still more congenial to him. Such lucidity and formality as are illustrated in the foregoing quotation, drawn ultimately from ancient models, were transformed by the "metaphysical" poets following Donne into a more sensitive and indigenous English verse, thus bestowing upon our poetry in general and upon Thoreau in particular the most charming of octosyllabic verse and a similarly fluid and controlled stanzaic structure. Marvell or some other poet of his times may be regarded as godfather to such a passage as the conclusion of "The River Swelleth More and More":

> Here Nature taught from year to year,
> When only red men came to hear;
> Methinks 'twas in this school of art
> Venice and Naples learned their part;
> But still their mistress, to my mind,
> Her young disciples leaves behind.

Marvell's school, with its metaphysical and subjective insight, also contributed an important part to the transcendental vision and lusty imagination of the New Englander. His inwardness appears notably in such a poem as "The Inward Morning." A highly fanciful symbolism ingeniously employed to express the mysteries of consciousness appears very much after the pattern of the "metaphysicals" in "Farewell," "Poverty," and "On Ponkawtasset, Since, We Took Our Way." The New Englander, with a realism exceeding Vaughan's, uses in "Upon This Bank at Early Dawn" the same bold and spiritualized image of the cock which Vaughan employs in his memorable "Cock-Crowing." The rigid architecture of the typical metaphysical poem also leaves an imprint on Thoreau's art, as may be seen in "I Knew a Man by Sight," with its stanzas in the most logical sequence possible. In one of the most nearly imitative of all his truly successful pieces,

"I Am a Parcel of Vain Strivings Tied," he comes strikingly close
to the verse forms of Herbert:

> I am a parcel of vain strivings tied
> By a chance bond together,
> Dangling this way and that, their links
> Were made so loose and wide,
> Methinks,
> For milder weather.

He became sensible to the charms of the baroque neoclassical
rhetoric of the age and school of James Thomson and William
Cowper. The poet who in one lyric employs the simplest and most
colloquial manner, in another assumes for gravity's sake the full
panoply of Augustan artifice and eloquence. He uses a heroic or
an epic diction in treating subjects where such a diction seems far
from inevitable. Yet here his warmth of feeling proves his salva-
tion. There is something genuinely poetic and instinctively noble
in his style, so that his poetry is seldom frozen into the rhetorical
frigidities which occasionally deface not only Lowell but Emerson.
"The Sluggish Smoke Curls up from Some Deep Dell" is a piece
by Thoreau in this pseudo-epic manner. Augustan robes, though
worn lightly, are still perceptible. This is his description of smoke
at dawn rising from a farmer's chimney.

> It has gone down the glen with the light wind,
> And o'er the plain unfurled its venturous wreath,
> Draped the tree tops, loitered upon the hill,
> And warmed the pinions of the early bird;
> And now, perchance, high in the crispy air,
> Has caught sight of the day o'er the earth's edge,
> And greets its master's eye at his low door,
> As some refulgent cloud in the upper sky.

Thoreau was kindled from the spiritual fires struck by the violence of the French Revolution upon the sterner and more mascu-
line of English minds, such as Blake's. The revolutionary temper,
so strong in Thoreau, found in the language of these earlier revo-
lutionaries an inspiration for his own poetic speech. There are
revolutionary explosives in the defiant poem which begins:

> The Good how can we trust?
> Only the Wise are just.

Several of his more reflective quatrains strike with an energy very similar to that of Blake. Again, in their faith and enthusiasm some of his most vigorous transcendental verses, as the superb lyric "All Things Are Current Found," bear the accent of spiritual assertion belonging to the more spiritual discoveries of the pioneers of the romantic movement.

Although Thoreau is never a strictly representative figure of either the earlier or later phases of romanticism, he naturally participates to a considerable degree in some of its major trends. An imagery finely descriptive of nature, a power in this imagery to beget a mood rich in emotion and vague in intellectual definition, as well as an audacious idealism show him a cousin, though not quite a brother, to the leading popular romantic poets in America and Europe. Thus while his remarkable poems on smoke and clouds bear the strongest marks of his own genius, they obviously stem from the main body of romantic nature verse. Notable in the same connection is his romantic fondness for autumn, almost as marked as in Corot. He wrote a cheerful nature lyric, "May Morning," Wordsworthian in its general intention though hardly in its execution, while the lines, "My Books I'd Fain Cast Off," praising nature above books, are also Wordsworthian in content though not in style. In "Walden" he dreams of nature before and after the Age of Man. The ethical phase of romanticism also affects him. One of his most notable flights of romantic idealism may be seen in the strongly imaginative lyric with the rather unfortunate first line, "Away! Away! Away! Away!"

Thoreau also participated in the rugged but somewhat strident didacticism which entered American poetry with Emerson and his immediate associates; and once more he reflected a movement without in any way losing his own individuality. Since he most nearly resembles Emerson yet differs from him notably, it becomes a nice test of Thoreau's art to place beside his own pieces Emerson's poems on like themes. Each poet, for example, wrote a fairly long ode on Mount Monadnock, alike not only in much of their imagery but in their ideas, language and, to a rather less degree, in rhythm. Yet the differences afford an excellent measurement of the general distinction between the two poets. Emerson's poem is clearer in meaning and nearer to the usual practices of the times in metre, symbol, texture, and total effect. A Yankee practicality in his verse withholds it from the more catholic and liberated imagination conspicuous in all Thoreau's best lyrics. To his contemporaries Thoreau's poem must certainly have appeared rough and raw. To us it seems less regular in its beauty, subtler, more meditative and, in the very delicacy and elusiveness of its symbolism, so much the more poetic. Thoreau's picture of mountains as ships pioneering on strange seas possesses a poetic scope and a richness of imagination of which Emerson proved incapable.

Thoreau as a poet flourished more in spiritual contact with past and future than with his own present. Hence the largest single group into which his chief poems fall, when considered historically, is that showing him in various ways anticipating the mind of the twentieth century. He touches the poetry of our own times closely largely in terms of its acute tensions. His verse, for example, often directly expresses the abrupt and vivid experience of the moment. Monuments to such sharp and intense experience appear in such pieces as "Music," "The Cliffs and Springs," and that unique poem on the imaginative import of unmusical sounds:

> They who prepare my evening meal below
> Carelessly hit the kettle as they go
> With tongs or shovel,
> And ringing round and round,
> Out of this hovel
> It makes an eastern temple by the sound.

A typical abruptness of phrase and boldness in sound connotative imagery may be seen in the first line of one of his lyrics, "Dong, sounds the brass in the East." The close and astringent conjunction of the concrete and the elusive, so much sought after in the poetry of the present age, may be seen in a poem comprised of six short lines:

> The waves slowly beat,
> Just to keep the noon sweet,
> And no sound is floated o'er,
> Save the mallet on shore,
> Which echoing on high
> Seems a-calking the sky.

As in much twentieth-century verse, nature imagery is first used to produce a mood and then suddenly surprises us by unveiling an imaginative idea, as when, in the lyric "Where Gleaming Fields of Haze," the "ancient" sound of the name "Souhegan" abruptly leads to thoughts of the Xanthus and Meander. The nervous heightening in subjectivity so keenly felt in much poetry of the twentieth century appears foreshadowed in the startling couplet at the end of "I Am the Autumnal Sun":

> And the rustling of the withered leaf
> Is the constant music of my grief.

Some less drastic features of modern verse making it appear more rugged than its nineteenth-century predecessor also give nerve and vigor to Thoreau's lines. These may be seen in bits of light but effective verse where humor comes to the support of idealism, or a homely realism to the aid of a lofty transcendentalism. "My Boots" and "Tall Ambrosia" offer instances. Finally, Thoreau's drastic and startling realistic satire in such highly acid poems as "For Though the Caves Were Rabitted" and "I Am the Little Irish Boy" resembles in a broad way the forthright manner of the brilliant satires of Yeats.

These powerful projections into the poetic mood of a restless age still almost a century in advance should free the scholar poet from any suspicion that he is merely imitative, overderivative, or immature. It is obviously true that as a young man he revolted from most contemporary fashions in letters as well as in life and gave himself to a devoted study of our heritage from Greece and Rome and from all the periods of the English literary record. But his scholarly habits were vitalizing habits, which happily added strength to his strongly creative mind and in no way fettered his creative faculties in chains of pedantic imitation. His scholarship is merely the outward sign of his universality as poet. His occasional lapses owing to bad taste may generally be ascribed to the limitations of his age, from which even so pronounced an individualist as he could not entirely escape. The refinements of his art, on the contrary, may best be discerned in his highly varied and modulated rhythms, his uncommonly flexible vocabulary and his many unclassifiable nuances. His strength is most intimately associated with his breadth. Thoreau found all schools of poetry his teachers, none his master. The publication at the present time is no accident. Thoreau's breadth of vision is precisely what our own age, tragically seeking a new consolidation of mankind, most of all requires.

[1946]

Henry Miller is the bad boy of contemporary American literature. His writings, whether novels, short stories, or essays, arouse controversy wherever they are read, and a number of them are banned from publication in this country. When he was asked to write a preface for a limited edition of Thoreau's three essays "Civil Disobedience," "Life Without Principle," and "A Plea for Captain John Brown," he broke through convention and scholarship, got down to the real marrow of Thoreau, and produced one of the most cogent and understanding interpretations of the politically-minded Thoreau to reach print.

PREFACE TO THREE ESSAYS BY HENRY DAVID THOREAU

BY HENRY MILLER

There are barely a half-dozen names in the history of America which have meaning for me. Thoreau's is one of them. I think of him as a true representative of America, a type, alas, which we have ceased to coin. He is not a democrat at all, in the sense we give to the word today. He is what Lawrence would call "an aristocrat of the spirit," which is to say, that rarest thing on earth: an individual. He is nearer to being an anarchist than a democrat, socialist or communist. However, he was not interested in politics; he was the sort of person who, if there were more of his kind, would soon cause governments to become non-existent. This, to my mind, is the highest type of man a community can pro-

---

From *Life Without Principle: Three Essays by Henry David Thoreau* (Stanford University: James Ladd Delkin, 1946), pp. i-viii.

duce. And that is why I have an unbounded respect and admiration for Thoreau.

The secret of his influence, which is still alive, still active, is a very simple one. He was a man of principle whose thought and behavior were in complete agreement. He assumed responsibility for his deeds as well as his utterances. Compromise was not in his vocabulary. America, for all her advantages, has produced only a handful of men of this calibre. The reason for it is obvious: men like Thoreau were never in agreement with the trend of the times. They symbolized that America which is as far from being born today as it was in 1776 or before. They took the hard road instead of the easy one. They believed in themselves first and foremost, they did not worry about what their neighbors thought of them, nor did they hesitate to defy the government when justice was at stake. There was never anything supine about their acquiescence: they could be wooed or seduced but not intimidated.

The essays gathered together in this little volume were all speeches, a fact of some importance if one reflects how impossible it would be today to give public utterance to such sentiments. The very notion of "civil disobedience," for example, is now unthinkable. (Except in India perhaps, where in his campaign of passive resistance Gandhi used this speech as a textbook.) In our country a man who dared to imitate Thoreau's behavior with regard to any crucial issue of the day would undoubtedly be sent to prison for life. Moreover, there would be none to defend him—as Thoreau once defended the name and reputation of John Brown. As always happens with bold, original utterances, these essays have now become classic. Which means that, though they still have the power to mould character, they no longer influence the men who govern our destiny. They are prescribed reading for students and a perpetual source of inspiration to the thinker and the rebel, but as for the reading public in general they carry no weight, no message any longer. The image of Thoreau has been fixed for the public by educators and "men of taste": it is that of a hermit, a crank, a nature faker. It is the caricature which has been preserved, as is usually the case with our eminent men.

The important thing about Thoreau, in my mind, is that he appeared at a time when we had, so to speak, a choice as to the direction we, the American people, would take. Like Emerson and Whitman, he pointed out the right road—the hard road, as I said before. As a people we chose differently. And we are now reaping the fruits of our choice. Thoreau, Whitman, Emerson—these men are now vindicated. In the gloom of current events these names stand out like beacons. We pay eloquent lip service to their memory, but we continue to flout their wisdom. We have become victims of the times; we look backward with longing and regret. It is too late now to change, we think. But it is not. As individuals, as men, it is never too late to change. That is precisely what these sturdy forerunners of ours were emphasizing all their lives.

With the creation of the atomic bomb, the whole world suddenly realizes that man is faced with a dilemma whose gravity is incommensurable. In the essay called "Life Without Principle," Thoreau anticipated that very possibility which shook the world when it received the news of the atomic bomb. "Of what consequence," says Thoreau, "though our planet explode, if there is no character involved in the explosion? . . . I would not run around a corner to see the world blow up."

I feel certain Thoreau would have kept his word, had the planet suddenly exploded of its own accord. But I also feel certain that, had he been told of the atomic bomb, of the good and bad that it was capable of producing, he would have had something memorable to say about its use. And he would have said it in defiance of the prevalent attitude. He would not have rejoiced that the secret of its manufacture was in the hands of the righteous ones. He would have asked immediately: "Who is righteous enough to employ such a diabolical instrument destructively?" He would have had no more faith in the wisdom and sanctity of this present government of the United States than he had of our government in the days of slavery. He died, let us not forget, in the midst of the Civil War, when the issue which should have been decided instantly by the conscience of every good citizen was at last being resolved in blood. No, Thoreau would have been the first to say that no government on earth is good enough or wise enough to be entrusted with such powers for good and evil. He would have predicted that we would use this new force in the same manner that we have used other natural forces, that the peace and security of the world lie not in inventions but in men's hearts, men's souls. His whole life bore testimony to the obvious fact which men are constantly overlooking, that to sustain life we need less rather than more, that to protect life we need courage and integrity, not weapons, not coalitions. In everything he said and did he was at the farthest remove from the man of today. I said earlier that his influence is still alive and active. It is, but only because truth and wisdom are incontrovertible and must eventually prevail. Consciously and unconsciously we are doing the very opposite of all that he advocated. But we are not happy about it, nor are we at all convinced that we are right. We are, in fact, more bewildered, more despairing, than we ever were in the course of our brief history. And that is most curious, most disturbing, since we are now acknowledged to be the most powerful, the most wealthy, the most secure of all the nations of the earth. We are at the top, but have we the vision to maintain this vantage point? We have a vague suspicion that we have been saddled with a responsibility which is too great for us. We know that we are not superior, in any real sense, to the other peoples of this earth. We are just waking up to the fact that morally we are far behind ourselves, so to speak. Some blissfully imagine that the threat of extinction—cosmic suicide—will rout us out of our lethargy. I am afraid that such dreams are doomed to be smashed even more effectively than the atom itself. Great things are not accomplished through fear of extinction. The deeds which move the world, which sustain life and give life, have a different motivation entirely.

The problem of power, an obsessive one with Americans, is now at the crux. Instead of *working* for peace, men ought to be urged to relax, to stop work, to take it easy, to dream and idle away their time for a change. Retire to the woods! if you can find any nearby. Think your own thoughts for a while! Examine your conscience, but only after you have thoroughly enjoyed yourself. What is your job worth, after all, if tomorrow you and yours can all be blown to smithereens by some reckless fool? Do you suppose that a government can be depended on any more than the separate individuals who compose it? Who are these individuals to whom the destiny of the planet itself now seems to be entrusted? Do you believe in them utterly, every one of them? What would *you* do if you had the control of this unheard of power? Would you use it for the benefit of all mankind, or just for your own people, or your own little group? Do you think that men can keep such a weighty secret to themselves? Do you think it *ought* to be kept secret?

These are the sort of questions I can imagine a Thoreau firing away. They are questions which, if one has just a bit of common sense, answer themselves. But governments never seem to possess this modicum of common sense. Nor do they trust those who are in possession of it.

"This American government—what is it but a tradition, though a recent one, endeavoring to transmit itself unimpaired to posterity, but each instant losing some of its integrity? It has not the vitality and force of a single living man; for a single man can bend it to his will. It is a sort of wooden gun to the people themselves. But it is not the less necessary for this; for the people must have some complicated machinery or other, and hear its din, to satisfy that idea of government which they have. Governments show thus how successfully men can be imposed on, even impose on themselves, for their own advantage. It is excellent, we must all allow. Yet this government never of itself furthered any enterprise, but by the alacrity with which it got out of its way. *It* does not keep the country free. *It* does not settle the West. *It* does not educate. The character inherent in the American people has done all that has been accomplished; and it would have done somewhat more, if the government had not sometimes got in its way. . . ."

That is the way Thoreau spoke a hundred years ago. He would speak still more unflatteringly if he were alive now. In these last hundred years the State has come to be a Frankenstein. We have **never** had less need of the State than now when we are most tyrannized by it. The ordinary citizen everywhere has a code of ethics far above that of the government to which he owes allegiance. The fiction that the State exists for our protection has been exploded a thousand times. However, as long as men lack self-assurance and self-reliance the State will thrive; it depends for its existence on the fear and uncertainty of its individual members.

By living his own life in his own "eccentric" way Thoreau demonstrated the futility and absurdity of the life of the (so-called) masses. It was a deep, rich life which yielded him the maximum of contentment. In the bare necessities he found adequate means for the enjoyment of life. "The opportunities of living," he pointed out, "are diminished in proportion as what are called the 'means' are increased." He was at home in Nature, where man belongs. He held communion with bird and beast, with plant and flower, with star and stream. He was not an unsocial being, far from it. He had friends, among women as well as men. No American has written more eloquently and truthfully of friendship than he. If his life seems a restricted one, it was a thousand times wider and deeper than the life of the ordinary American today. He lost nothing by not mingling with the crowd, by not devouring the newspapers, by not enjoying the radio or the movies, by not having an automobile, a refrigerator, a vacuum cleaner. He not only did not lose anything through the lack of these things but he actually enriched himself in a way far beyond the ability of the man of today who is glutted with these dubious comforts and conveniences. Thoreau lived, whereas we may be said to barely exist. In power and depth, his thought not only matches that of our contemporaries, but usually surpasses it. In courage and virtue there are none among our leading spirits today to match him. As a writer, he is among the first three or four we can boast of. Viewed now from the heights of our decadence, he seems almost like an early Roman. The word virtue has meaning again, when connected with his name.

It is the young people of America who may profit from his homely wisdom, from his example even more. They need to be reassured that what was possible then is still possible today.

America is still, a vastly unpopulated country, a land abounding in forests, streams, lakes, deserts, mountains, prairies, rivers, where a man of good-will with a little effort and belief in his own powers can enjoy a deep, tranquil, rich life—provided he go his own way. He need not and should not think of making a good living, but rather of creating a good life for himself. The wise men always return to the soil; one has only to think of the great men of India, China and France, their poets, sages, artists, to realize how deep is this need in every man. I am thinking, naturally, of creative types, for the others will gravitate to their own unimaginative levels, never suspecting that life holds any better promise. I think of the budding American poets, sages and artists because they appear so appallingly helpless in this present-day American world. They all wonder so naively how they will live if they do not hire themselves out to some task-master; they wonder still more how, after doing that, they will ever find time to do what they were called to do. They never think any more of going into the desert or the wilderness, of wresting a living from the soil, of doing odd jobs, of living on as little as possible. They remain in the towns and cities, flitting from one thing to another, restless, miserable, frustrated, searching in vain for a way out. They ought to be told at the outset that society, as it is now constituted, provides no way out, that the solution is in their own hands and that it can be won only by the use of their own two hands. One has to hack his way out with the axe. The real wilderness is not out there somewhere, but in the towns and cities, in that complicated web which we have made of life and which serves no purpose but to thwart, cramp and inhibit the free spirits. Let a man believe in himself and he will find a way to exist despite the barriers and traditions which hem him in. The America of Thoreau's day was just as contemptuous of, just as hostile to, his experiment as we are today to any one who essays it. Undeveloped as the country was then, men were lured from all regions, all walks of life, by the discovery of gold in California. Thoreau stayed at home where he cultivated his own mine. He had only to go a few miles to be deep in the heart of Nature. For most of us, no matter where we live in this great country, it is still possible to travel but a few miles and find oneself in Nature. I have travelled the length and breadth of the land, and if I was impressed by one thing it was by this—that America is empty. It is also true, to be sure, that nearly all this empty space is owned by some one or other— banks, railroads, insurance companies and so on. It is almost impossible to wander off the beaten path without "trespassing" on private property. But that nonsense would soon cease if people began to get up on their hind legs and desert the towns and cities. John Brown and a bare handful of men virtually defeated the entire population of America. It was the Abolitionists who freed the slaves, not the armies of Grant and Sherman, not Abraham Lincoln. There is no ideal condition of life to step into anywhere at any time. Everything is difficult, and everything becomes more difficult still when you choose to live your own life. But, to live one's own life is still the best way of life, always was, and always will be. The greatest snare and delusion is to postpone living your own life until an ideal form of government is created which will permit every one to lead the good life. Lead the good life now, this instant, every instant, to the best of your ability and you will bring about indirectly and unconsciously a form of government nearer to the ideal.

Because Thoreau laid such emphasis on conscience and on active resistance, one is apt to think of his life as bare and grim. One forgets that he was a man who shunned work as much as possible, who knew how to idle his time away. Stern moralist that he was, he had nothing in common with the professional moralists. He was too deeply religious to have anything to do with the Church, just as he was too much the man of action to bother with politics. Similarly he was too rich in spirit to think of amassing wealth, too courageous, too self-reliant, to worry about security and protection. He found, by opening his eyes, that life provides everything necessary for man's peace and enjoyment—one has only to make use of what is there, ready to hand as it were. "Life is bountiful," he seems to be saying all the time. *"Relax! Life is here, all about you, not there, not over the hill."*

He found Walden. But Walden is everywhere, if the man himself is there. Walden has become a symbol. It should become a reality. Thoreau himself has become a symbol. But he was only a man, let us not forget that. By making him a symbol, by raising memorials to him, we defeat the very purpose of his life. Only by living our own lives to the full can we honor his memory. We should not try to imitate him but to surpass him. Each one of us has a totally different life to lead. We should not strive to become like Thoreau, nor even like Jesus Christ, but to become what we are in truth and in essence. That is the message of every great individual and the whole meaning of being an individual. To be anything less is to move nearer to nullity.

[1946]

It would indeed be shortsighted not to include a Freudian insight into Thoreau. But, strangely enough, the psychologists and psychiatrists have pretty much left his work alone. One of the nearest approaches is that of the young critic Stanley Hyman. It aroused a great deal of discussion among the Thoreau disciples, most of whom thought (as might be expected) that Mr. Hyman read more into the symbolism of Walden *than was there. On the whole they tended to ignore the fact that Mr. Hyman's essay was one of the most thoughtful of his time.*

HENRY THOREAU IN OUR TIME

BY STANLEY EDGAR HYMAN

1

In July, 1945, we celebrated the centennial of Henry David Thoreau's retirement to Walden Pond. Almost twice as many old ladies as usual made the pilgrimage to Concord, to see the shrine containing his furniture, and to Walden, where they had the privilege of adding a rock to the cairn where his hut once stood and of opening a box lunch in the picnic ground that stands as his monument. The American Museum of Natural History staged a Walden Pond exhibit. The *Saturday Evening Post* ran an illustrated article. And to add the final mortuary touch, a professor of English published a slim volume called *Walden Revisited*. All in all, it was a typical American literary centennial. Henry Thoreau would probably not have enjoyed it.

From *Atlantic Monthly*, CLXXVIII (November, 1946), 137-46, by permission.

A more significant Thoreau centenary would have been July, 1946, the hundredth anniversary of his going to jail. Every reader of *Walden* knows the story. Thoreau had not paid a poll tax for several years, as a sign that he had renounced his allegiance to a government that protected slavery and made war on Mexico, and one day when he walked into Concord to get a mended shoe from the cobbler he was seized and put into jail. That night the tax was paid for him, and the next morning he was freed, obtained his mended shoe, and went back to the woods to pick some berries for dinner. While he was in jail, placidly meditating on the nature of state coercion, Emerson is supposed to have come by and asked: "Henry, what are you doing in *there?*" To which Thoreau is supposed to have replied. "Waldo, what are *you* doing *out there?*"

It takes not much investigation into the story to discover that the actual details of Thoreau's first great political gesture were largely ridiculous. For one thing, the act itself was both safe and imitative, Bronson Alcott having given Thoreau the idea three years before by refusing to pay his taxes and going to jail, where he was treated quite well. For another, Thoreau in jail seems to have been not at all the philosophic muser he makes himself out to be, but, as the jailer later reported, "mad as the devil." For a third, Emerson certainly engaged in no such pat dialogue with him, for the jailer allowed no visitors, and Emerson's actual reaction to the event was to tell Alcott he thought it was "mean and skulking, and in bad taste." Finally, the person who "interfered" and paid his tax was Thoreau's old Aunt Maria, disguised with a shawl over her head so that Henry would not be angry with her for spoiling his gesture.

Why, then, celebrate the centenary of this absurd event? For only one reason. As a political warrior, Thoreau was a comic little figure with a receding chin, and not enough high style to carry off a gesture. As a political writer, he was the most ringing and magnificent polemicist America has ever produced. Three years later he made an essay called *Civil Disobedience* out of his prison experience, fusing the soft coal of his night in jail into solid diamond. *Civil Disobedience* has all the power and dignity that Thoreau's political act so signally lacked. "Under a government which imprisons any unjustly, the true place for a just man is also a prison," he writes in a line Debs later echoed, ". . . the only home in a slave state in which a free man can abide with honor." "I saw that the State was halfwitted, that it was timid as a lone woman with her silver spoons, and that it did not know its friends from it foes, and I lost all my remaining respect for it, and pitied it." He summarizes his position reasonably, even humorously, but with finality:—

I have never declined paying the highway tax, because I am as desirous of being a good neighbor as I am of being a bad subject; and as for supporting schools, I am doing my part to educate my fellowcountrymen now. It is for no particular item in the tax-bill that I refuse to pay it. I simply wish to refuse allegiance to the State, to withdraw and stand aloof from it effectually. I do not care to trace the course of my dollar, if I could, till it buys a man or a musket to shoot with, — the dollar is innocent, — but I am concerned to trace the effects of my allegiance. In fact, I quietly declare war with the State, after my fashion, though I will still make what use and get what advantage of her I can, as is usual in such cases.

In the relative futility of Thoreau's political act and the real importance of his political essay based on it, we have an allegory for our time on the artist as politician: the artist as strong and serviceable in the earnest practice of his art as he is weak and faintly comic in direct political action. In a day when the pressure on the artist to forsake his art for his duties as a citizen is almost irresistible, when every painter is making posters on nutrition, when every composer is founding a society devoted to doing something about the atom bomb, when every writer is spending more time on committees than on the typewriter, we can use Henry Thoreau's example.

In the past century we have had various cockeyed and contradictory readings of Thoreau's "essence." But from them we can reach two conclusions. One is that he is probably a subtler and more ambiguous character than anyone seems to have noticed. The other is that he must somehow still retain a powerful magic or there would not be such a need to capture or destroy him, to canonize the shade or weight it down in the earth under a cairn of rocks. It is obvious that we shall have to create a Thoreau for ourselves.

The first thing we should insist on is that Thoreau was a writer, not a man who lived in the woods or didn't pay taxes or went to jail. At his best he wrote the only really first-rate prose ever written by an American, with the possible exception of Abraham Lincoln. The *Plea for Captain John Brown,* his most sustained lyric work, rings like *Areopagitica,* and like *Areopagitica* it is the product of passion combined with complete technical mastery. Here are two sentences:—

> The momentary charge at Balaklava, in obedience to a blundering command, proving what a perfect machine the soldier is, has, properly enough, been celebrated by a poet laureate; but the steady, and for the most part successful, charge of this man, for some years, against the legions of Slavery, in obedience to an infinitely higher command, is as much more memorable than that as an intelligent and conscientious man is superior to a machine. Do you think that that will go unsung?

Thoreau was not only a writer, but a writer in the great stream of the American tradition, the mythic and non-realist writers, Hawthorne and Melville, Mark Twain and Henry James, and, in our own day, as Malcolm Cowley has been most insistent in pointing out, Hemingway and Faulkner. In pointing out Hemingway's kinship, not to our relatively barren realists and naturalists, but to our "haunted and nocturnal writers, the men who dealt in images that were symbols of an inner world," Cowley demonstrates that the idyllic fishing landscape of such a story as "Big Two-Hearted River" is not a real landscape setting for a real fishing trip, but an enchanted landscape full of rituals and taboos, a metaphor or projection of an inner state.

It would not be hard to demonstrate the same thing for the landscape in *Walden.* One defender of such a view would be Henry Thoreau, who writes in his *Journals,* along with innumerable tributes to the power of mythology, that the richest function of nature is to symbolize human life, to become fable and myth for man's inward experience. F. O. Matthiessen, probably the best critic we have devoting himself to American literature, has claimed that Thoreau's power lies precisely in his re-creation of basic myth, in his role as the protagonist in a great cyclic ritual drama.

2

Central to any interpretation of Thoreau is Walden, both the experience of living by the pond and the book that reported it. As he explains it in the book, it was an experiment in human ecology (and if Thoreau was a scientist in any field, it was ecology, though he preceded the term), an attempt to work out a satisfactory relationship between man and his environment. He writes:—

> I went to the woods because I wished to live deliberately, to front only the essential facts of life, and see if I could not learn what it had to teach, and not, when I came to die, discover that I had not lived. I did not wish to live what was not life, living is so dear; nor did I wish to practice resignation, unless it was quite necessary. I wanted to live deep and suck out all the marrow of life, to live so sturdily and Spartan-like as to put to rout all that was not life, to cut a broad swath and shave close, to drive life into a corner, and reduce it to its lowest terms, and, if it proved to be mean, why then to get the whole and genuine meanness of it, and publish its meanness to the world; or if it were sublime, to know it by experience, and be able to give a true account of it in my next excursion.

And of his leaving:—

> I left the woods for as good a reason as I went there. Perhaps it seemed to me that I had several more lives to live, and could not spare any more time for that one.

At Walden, Thoreau reports the experience of awakening one morning with the sense that some question had been put to him, which he had been endeavoring in vain to answer in his sleep. In his terms, that question would be the problem with which he begins *Life Without Principle:* "Let us consider the way in which we spend our lives." His obsessive image, running through everything he ever wrote, is the myth of Apollo, glorious god of the sun, forced to labor on earth tending the flocks of King Admetus. In one sense, of course, the picture of Henry Thoreau forced to tend anyone's flocks is ironic, and Stevenson is right when he notes sarcastically: "Admetus never got less work out of any servant since the world began." In another sense the myth has a basic rightness, and is, like the Pied Piper of Hamelin, an archetypal allegory of the artist in a society that gives him no worthy function and no commensurate reward.

The sun is Thoreau's key symbol, and all of *Walden* is a development in the ambiguities of sun imagery. The book begins with the theme: "But alert and healthy natures remember that the sun rose clear," and ends: "There is more day to dawn. The sun is but a morning star." Thoreau's movement from an egocentric to a sociocentric view is the movement from "I have, as it were, my own sun, and moon, and stars, and a little world all to myself" to "The same sun which ripens my beans illumines at once a system of earths like ours." The sun is an old Platonist like Emerson that must set before Thoreau's true sun can rise; it is menaced by every variety of mist, haze, smoke, and darkness; it is Thoreau's brother; it is both his own cold affection and the threat of sensuality that would corrupt goodness as it taints meat; it is himself in a pun on s-o-n, s-u-n.

When Abolitionism becomes a nagging demand Thoreau can no longer resist, a Negro woman is a dusky orb rising on Concord, and when John Brown finally strikes his blow for Thoreau the sun shines on him, and he works "in the clearest light that shines on the land." The final announcement of Thoreau's triumphant rebirth at Walden is the sun breaking through mists. It is not to our purpose here to explore the deep and complex ambiguities of Thoreau's sun symbol, or in fact to do more than note a few of many contexts, but no one can study the sun references in *Walden* without realizing that Thoreau is a deeper and more complicated writer than we have been told, and that the book is essentially dynamic rather than static, a movement *from* something *to* something, rather than simple reporting of an experience.

Walden is, in fact, a vast rebirth ritual, the purest and most complete in our literature. We know rebirth rituals to operate characteristically by means of fire, ice or decay, mountains and pits, but we are staggered by the amount and variety of these in the book. We see Thoreau build his shanty of boards he has first purified in the sun, record approvingly an Indian purification ritual of burning all the tribe's old belongings and provisions, and later go off into a description of the way he is cleansed and renewed by his own fireplace. We see him note the magic purity of the ice on Walden Pond, the fact that frozen water never turns stale, and the rebirth involved when the ice breaks up, all sins are forgiven, and "Walden was dead and is alive again." We see him exploring every phase and type of decay: rotting ice, decaying trees, moldy pitch pine and rotten wood, excrement, maggots, a vulture feeding on a dead horse, carrion, tainted meat, and putrid water.

The whole of *Walden* runs to symbols of graves and coffins, with consequent rising from them, to wombs and emergence from them, and ends on the fable of a live insect resurrected from an egg long buried in wood. Each day at Walden Thoreau was reborn by his bath in the pond, a religious exercise he says he took for purification and renewal, and the whole two years and two months he compresses into the cycle of a year, to frame the book on the basic rebirth pattern of the death and renewal of vegetation, ending it with the magical emergence of spring.

On the thread of decay and rebirth Thoreau strings all his preoccupations. Meat is a symbol of evil, sensuality; its tainting symbolizes goodness and affection corrupted; the shameful defilement of chastity smells like carrion (in which he agreed with Shakespeare); the eating of meat causes slavery and unjust war. (Thoreau, who was a vegetarian, sometimes felt so wild he was tempted to seize and devour a woodchuck raw, or yearned like a savage for the raw marrow of kudus—those were the periods when he wanted to seize the world by the neck and hold it under water like a dog until it drowned.)

But even slavery and injustice are a decaying and a death, and Thoreau concludes *Slavery in Massachusetts* with: "We do not complain that they *live,* but that they do not *get buried.* Let the living bury them; even they are good for manure." Always, in Thoreau's imagery, what this rotting meat will fertilize is fruit, ripe fruit. It is his chief good. He wanted "the flower and fruit of man," the "ripeness." The perfect and glorious state he foresees will bear men as fruit, suffering them to drop off as they ripen; John Brown's heroism is a good seed that will bear good fruit, a future crop of heroes. Just as Brown, in one of the most terrifying puns ever written, was "ripe" for the gallows, Thoreau reports after writing *Civil Disobedience,* as he dwells on action and wildness, that he feels ripe, fertile: "It is seedtime with me. I have lain fallow long enough." On the metaphor of the organic process of birth, growth, decay, and rebirth out of decay, Thoreau organizes his whole life and experience.

I have maintained that *Walden* is a dynamic process, a job of symbolic action, a moving *from* something *to* something. From what to what? On an abstract level, from individual isolation to collective identification—from, in Macaulay's terms, a Platonic philosophy of pure truth to a Baconian philosophy of use. It is interesting to note that the term Bacon used for the utilitarian ends of knowledge, for the relief of man's estate, is "fruit." The Thoreau who went to Walden was a pure Platonist, a man who could review a Utopian book and announce that it was too practical, that its chief fault was aiming "to secure the greatest degree of gross comfort and pleasure merely." The man who left Walden was the man who thought it was less important for John Brown to right a Greek accent slanting the wrong way than to right a falling slave.

Early in the book Thoreau gives us his famous Platonic myth of having long ago lost a hound, a bay horse, and a turtle dove. Before he is through, his symbolic quest is for a human being, and near the end of the book he reports of a hunter: "He had lost a dog but found a man." All through *Walden* he weighs Platonic and Baconian values: men keep chickens for the glorious sound of a crowing cock "to say nothing of the eggs and drumsticks"; a well reminds a man of the insignificance of his dry pursuits on a surface largely water, and also keeps the butter cool. By the end of the book he has brought Transcendentalism down to earth, has taken Emerson's castles in the air, to use his own figure, and built foundations under them.

3

Thoreau's political value, for us, is largely in terms of this transition from philosophic aloofness. We see in him the honest artist struggling for terms on which he can adjust to society *in his capacity as artist*. As might be expected from such a process, Thoreau's social statements are full of contradictions, and quotations can be amputated from the context of his work to bolster any position from absolute anarchism to ultimate toryism, if indeed they are very far apart. At his worst, he is simply a nut reformer, one of the horde in his period, attempting to "improve" an Irish neighbor by lecturing him on abstinence from tea, coffee, and meat as the solution to all his problems, and the passage in *Walden* describing his experience is the most condescending and offensive in a sometimes infuriating book. At his best, he is the clearest voice for social ethics that ever spoke out in America.

One of the inevitable consequences of Emersonian idealism was the ease with which it could be used to sugar-coat social injustice, as a later generation was to discover when it saw robber barons piling up fortunes while intoning Emersonian slogans of Self-Reliance and Compensation. If the Lowell factory owner was more enslaved than one of his child laborers, there was little point in seeking to improve the lot of the child laborer, and frequently Emerson seemed to be preaching a principle that would forbid both the rich and the poor to sleep under bridges. Thoreau begins *Walden* in these terms, remarking that it is frivolous to attend to "the gross but somewhat foreign form of servitude called Negro Slavery when there are so many keen and subtle masters that enslave"; that the rich are a "seemingly wealthy, but most terribly impoverished class of all," since they are fettered by their gold and silver; that the day laborer is more independent than his employer, since his day ends with sundown, while his employer has no respite from one year to another; even that if you give a ragged man money he will perhaps buy more rags with it, since he is frequently gross, with a taste for rags.

Against this ingenious and certainly unintentional social palliation, *Walden* works through to sharp social criticism: of the New England textile factory system, whose object is, "not that mankind may be well and honestly clad, but, unquestionably, that the corporations may be enriched"; of the degradation of the laboring class of his time, "living in sties," shrunken in mind and body; of the worse condition of the Southern slaves; of the lack of dignity and privacy in the lives of factory girls, "never alone, hardly in their dreams"; of the human consequences of commerce and technology; of the greed and corruption of the money-mad New England of his day, seeing the whole world in the bright reflecting surface of a dollar.

As his bitterness and awareness increased, Thoreau's direct action became transmuted. He had always, like his friends and family, helped the Underground Railway run escaped slaves to Canada. He devotes a sentence to one such experience in *Walden,* and amplifies it in his *Journal,* turning a quiet and terrible irony on the man's attempt to buy his freedom from his master, who was his father, and exercised paternal love by holding out for more than the slave could pay. These actions, however, in a man who disliked Abolitionism, seem to have been simple reflexes of common decency, against his principles, which would free the slave first by striking off his spiritual chains.

From this view, Thoreau works tortuously through to his final identification of John Brown, the quintessence of direct social action, with all beauty, music, poetry, philosophy, and Christianity. Finally Brown becomes Christ, an indignant militant who cleansed the temple, preached radical doctrines, and was crucified by the slaveowners. In what amounts almost to worship of Brown, Thoreau both deifies the action he had tried to avoid and transcends it in passion. Brown died for him, thus he need free no more slaves.

At the same time, Thoreau fought his way through the Emersonian doctrine that a man might wash his hands of wrong, providing he did not himself commit it. He writes in *Civil Disobedience:*—

> It is not a man's duty, as a matter of course, to devote himself to the eradication of any, even the most enormous wrong; he may still properly have other concerns to engage him; but it is his duty, at least, to wash his hands of it, and, if he gives it no thought longer, not to give it practically his support. If I devote myself to other pursuits and contemplations, I must first see, at least, that I do not pursue them sitting upon another man's shoulders. I must get off him first, that he may pursue his contemplations too.

Here he has recognized the fallacy of the Greek philosopher, free because he is supported by the labor of slaves, and the logic of this realization was to drive him, through the superiority and smugness of "God does not sympathize with the popular movements," and "I came into this world, not chiefly to make this a good place to live in, but to live in it, be it good or bad," to the militant fury of "My thoughts are murder to the State, and involuntarily go plotting against her."

Thoreau's progress also involved transcending his economics. The first chapter of *Walden,* entitled "Economy," is an elaborate attempt to justify his life and views in the money terms of New England commerce. He speaks of going to the woods as "going into business" on "slender capital," of his "enterprise"; gives the reader his "accounts," even to the halfpenny, of what he spends and what he takes in; talks of "buying dear," of "paying compound interest." He accepts the ledger principle, though he sneaks into the Credit category such unusual profits on his investment as "leisure and independence and health." His money metaphor begins to break down when he writes of the Massachusetts citizens who read of the unjust war against Mexico as sleepily as they read the prices-current, and he cries out: "What is the price-current of an honest man and patriot today?" By the time of the John Brown affair he has evolved two absolutely independent economies, a money economy and a moral economy. He writes:—

"But he won't gain anything by it." Well, no, I don't suppose he could get four-and-sixpence a day for being hung, take the year round; but then he stands a chance to save a considerable part of his soul, — and *such* a soul! — when you do not. No doubt you can get more in your market for a quart of milk than for a quart of blood, but that is not the market that heroes carry their blood to.

What, then, can we make of this complicated social pattern? Following Emerson's doctrine and example, Thoreau was frequently freely inconsistent. One of his chief contradictions was on the matter of reforming the world through his example. He could disclaim hoping to influence anyone with "I do not mean to prescribe rules to strong and valiant natures" and then take it back immediately with "I foresee that all men will at length establish their lives on that basis." Certainly to us his hatred of technological progress, of the division of labor, even of farming with draft animals and fertilizer, is backward-looking and reactionary. Certainly he distrusted cooperative action and all organization. But the example of Jefferson reminds us that a man may be economically backward-looking and still be our noblest spokesman, just as Hamilton reminds us that a man may bring us reaction and injustice tied up in the bright tissue of economic progress.

To the doctrine of naked expediency so tempting to our time, the worship of power and success for which the James Burnhams among us speak so plausibly, Thoreau opposes only one weapon—principle. Not policy or expediency must be the test, but justice and principle. "Read not the Times, read the Eternities." *Walden* has been a bible for the British labor movement since the days of William Morris. We might wonder what the British Labor Party, now that it is in power, or the rest of us, in and out of power, who claim to speak for principle, would make of Thoreau's doctrine: "If I have unjustly wrested a plank from a drowning man, I must restore it to him though I drown myself."

4

All of this takes us far afield from what must be Thoreau's chief importance to us, his writing. The resources of his craft warrant our study. One of his most eloquent devices, typified by the crack about the Times and the Eternities, is a root use of words, resulting from his lifelong interest in language and etymology, fresh, shocking, and very close to the pun. We can see the etymological passion developing in the *Journal* notes that a "wild" man is actually a "willed" man, that our "fields" are "felled" woods. His early writings keep reminding us that a "saunterer" is going to a "Sainte Terre," a Holy Land; that three roads can make a village "trivial"; that when our center is outside us we are "eccentric"; that a "landlord" is literally a "lord of the land"; that he has been "breaking" silence for years and has hardly made a "rent" in it.

By the time he wrote *Walden* this habit had developed into one of his most characteristic ironic devices: the insistence that telling his townsmen about his life is not "impertinent" but "pertinent," that professors of philosophy are not philosophers, but people who "profess" it, that the "bent" of his genius is a very "crooked" one. In the *Plea for Captain John Brown* the device rises to a whiplash power. He says that Brown's "humanities" were the freeing of slaves, not the study of grammar; that a Board of Commissions is lumber of which he had only lately heard; of the Governor of Massachusetts: "He was no Governor of mine. He did not govern me." Sometimes these puns double and triple to permit him to pack a number of complex meanings into a single word, like the "dear" in "Living is so dear." The discord of goose-honk and owl-cry he hears by the pond becomes a "concord" that is at once musical harmony, his native town, and concord as "peace."

Closely related to these serious puns in Thoreau is a serious epigrammatic humor—wry, quotable lines which contain a good deal of meaning and tend to make their point by shifting linguistic levels. "Some circumstantial evidence is very strong, as when you find a trout in the milk." To a man who threatened to plumb his depths: "I trust you will not strike your head against the bottom." "The partridge loves peas, but not those that go with her into the pot." On his habit of exaggeration: "You must speak loud to those who are hard of hearing."

He reported that the question he feared was not "How much wood did you burn?" but "What did you do while you were warm?" Dying, to someone who wanted to talk about the next world: "One world at a time"; and to another, who asked whether he had made his peace with God: "We have never quarrelled." When Emerson remarked that they taught all branches of learning at Harvard: "All of the branches and none of the roots." Refusing to pay a dollar for his Harvard diploma: "Let every sheep keep but his own skin." Asked to write for the *Ladies' Companion:* "I could not write anything companionable." Many of these are variants of the same joke, and in a few cases, the humor is sour and forced, like the definition of a pearl as "the hardened tear of a diseased clam, murdered in its old age," or a soldier as "a fool made conspicuous by a painted coat." But those are penalties any man who works for humor must occasionally pay, and Thoreau believed this "indispensable pledge of sanity" to be so important that without some leaven of it "the abstruse thinker may justly be suspected of mysticism, fanaticism or insanity." "Especially the transcendental philosophy needs the leaven of humor," he wrote, in what must go down as understatement.

Thoreau was perhaps more precise about his own style and more preoccupied generally with literary craft than any American writer except Henry James. He rewrote endlessly, not only, like James, for greater precision, but unlike James, for greater simplicity. "Simplify, Simplify, Simplify," he gave as the three cardinal principles of both life and art. Emerson had said of Montaigne: "Cut these words and they would bleed," and Thoreau's is perhaps the only American style in his century of which this is true. Criticizing De Quincey, he stated his own prose aesthetic, "the *art* of writing," demanding sentences that are concentrated and nutty, that suggest far more than they say, that are kinked and knotted into something hard and significant, to be swallowed like a diamond without digesting. "Sentences which are expensive, towards which so many volumes, so much life, went; which lie like boulders on the page, up and down or across; which contain the seed of other sentences, not mere repetition, but creation; which a man might sell his grounds and castles to build."

In another place he notes that writing must be done with gusto, must be vascular. A sense of Thoreau's preoccupation with craft comes with noting that when he lists "My faults" in the *Journal,* all seven of them turn out to be of his prose style. Writing for Thoreau was so obsessive, so vital a physical process, that at various times he describes it in the imagery of eating, procreation, excretion, mystic trance, and even his old favorite, the tree bearing ripe fruit. An anthology of Thoreau's passages on the art of writing would be as worth compiling as Henry James's prefaces and certainly as useful to both the writer and the reader.

Thoreau's somewhat granite pride and aloofness are at their most appealing, and very like James Joyce's, when he is defending his manuscripts against editorial bowdlerizing, when he stands as the embattled writer against the phalanx of cowardice and stupidity. He fought Emerson and Margaret Fuller on a line in one of his poems they printed in the *Dial,* and won. When the editor of *Putnam's Monthly* cut passages from an article, Thoreau wrote to a friend: "The editor requires the liberty to omit the heresies without consulting me, a privilege California is not rich enough to bid for," and withdrew the series. His letter to Lowell, the editor of the *Atlantic,* when Lowell cut a "pantheistic" sentence out of cowardice, is a masterpiece of bitter fury, withering Lowell like a premature bud in a blast.

Henry Thoreau's and John Brown's personalities were as different as any two personalities can be; one the gentle, rather shy scholar who took children huckleberrying, the other the harsh military Puritan who could murder the children of slavers in cold blood on the Potawatomie, with the fearful statement: "Nits grow to be lice." Almost the only things they had in common, that made Thoreau perceive that Brown was his man, his ideas in action, almost his Redeemer, were principle and literary style. Just as writers in our own day were drawn to Sacco and Vanzetti perhaps as much for the majesty of Vanzetti's untutored prose as for the obvious justice of their case, Thoreau somehow found the most convincing thing about Brown to be his speech to the court. At the end of his *Plea* he quotes Brown's "sweet and noble strain":—

> I pity the poor in bondage that have none to help them; that is why I am here; not to gratify any personal animosity, revenge, or vindictive spirit. It is my sympathy with the oppressed and the wronged, that are as good as you, and as precious in the sight of God.

adding only: "You don't know your testament when you see it."

"This unlettered man's speaking and writing are standard English," he writes in another paper on Brown. "It suggests that the one great rule of composition—and if I were a professor of rhetoric I should insist on this—is, to *speak the truth.*" It was certainly Thoreau's great rule of composition. "He was a speaker and actor of the truth," Emerson said in his obituary of Thoreau. We have never had too many of those. He was also, perhaps as a consequence, a very great writer. We have never had too many of those, either.

[1951]

When the fourteen-volume edition of Thoreau's Journals was re-issued recently, after having been out of print for forty years, it gave our literary critics an opportunity to re-evaluate Thoreau. One of the best of these re-evaluations was by the young Alfred Kazin, who a few years before had so widely impressed the literary world with his volume of criticism, On Native Grounds.

THOREAU'S JOURNALS

BY ALFRED KAZIN

Many writers have kept journals—the habit is almost an occupational necessity. It was in America once a characteristic literary and moralistic exercise by no means confined to New England Puritans and seems to have become a favorite literary practice in France. Some writers, like Emerson, have kept their journals as a "savings bank" for future work; some, like Dostoevsky and François Mauriac, in the form of newspaper polemics; some, like Amiel, as an apology for their failure in the world; some—Andre Gide is now the most fascinating contemporary example—have kept theirs as artful public confessions, and, in the usual self-conscious twentieth-century way, with more emphasis on their longing for sincerity than on the truth itself.

But even among writers' journals—and usually, with the exception of dry business-like records like Benjamin Constant's and Arnold Bennett's, each is as interesting as the man who kept it—Thoreau's must stand in a special place. For his journal—now reprinted for the first time since the edition of 1906 long out of

From *New York Herald Tribune Books,* May 20, 1951.

print—is not merely the record of a life lived almost entirely within. It is the life itself. Thoreau's Journal was not a hide-out for his lacerated soul, not altogether what he and others have most used it for—the storehouse out of which his published books would come. It was the thing he lived in, the containment of his love—and therefore had to be as well-written as a prayer or a love letter. "All that a man has to say or do that can possibly concern mankind," he found himself writing in 1854, "is in some shape or other to tell the story of his love—to sing; and, if he is fortunate and keeps alive, he will be forever in love. This alone is to be alive to the extremities." This is where he sang, sentence by sentence; the journal took its "shape" from the manner of his love.

Actually, the Journal bogs down after the middle volumes into disjointed nature notes of whose barrenness even as scientific information he was well aware. But it is the unflagging beauty of the writing, day after day, that confirms its greatness among writers' journals. It is not natural for a man to write this well every day. Only a man who had no other life but to practice a particularly intense and truthful kind of prose could have done it—a man for whom all walks finally came to end in the hard athletic sentence that would recover all their excitement. Other writers have been lonely, and have learned to accept their loneliness; have felt yearnings toward God that their distrust of churches could not explain; have dissected their solitary characters down to the last bearable foundation in human self-analysis; have, at least in the privacy of a journal, scored off at last the obtuseness of their neighbors, the insipidity of their contemporaries and the unfeelingness of the age. And of course all writers of memorable journals have made characters out of themselves; you have to be thoroughly suffused in yourself before you can break away and take a good look back. Thoreau did all this, and something more. For in and through his Journal he finally made himself a prose that would fully evoke in its resonant tension and wildness the life he lived in himself every day.

The Journal was begun when he was twenty, a few months out

of Harvard, and noted that someone (Emerson?) had asked him: "What are you doing now? Do you keep a journal?" "So I make my first entry today." He concluded it thirty-nine manuscript volumes later, in 1861, when his last illness made impossible those daily afternoon walks that were the sustenance of all his literary work. The first volume, whose opening pages suggest the commonplace book he must have kept at college, is earnestly packed with quotations from Latin, Greek and German writers, his early poems, and those tiresomely sententious aphorisms and "analogies" between nature and man's spiritual life in which he was still consciously modelling himself after Emerson, but which were always to be the weakest and actually least characteristic element in his writing. But soon the journal settles down into the pattern of those walks—"to Conantum," "to Fair Haven," "to Walden"—on which he kept field notes he later carefully rewrote and extended into his Journal.

There is very little in it of how he earned his living—as a handy man in Emerson's household, as a pencil maker, as a lecturer; something more, in the middle volumes, since the occupation was so congenial to him, on his experiences as a surveyor. Nor is it from the Journal that you would learn that he interrupted his stay at Walden to go to jail for a night because of his refusal to pay a poll-tax to support the Mexican War; or that it was he who rang the bell of Concord's Town Hall when not even the sexton would do it, to announce Emerson's discourse in 1844 on the emancipation of the slaves in the West Indies; or *whom* it was he ever loved—only that he had so ideal a conception of friendship and love that no genuine experiences could ever have satisfied him. From time to time there are shrewd, rather too self-righteous, sometimes disdainful, but not altogether unaffectionate notes on his neighbors in Concord, on the farmers around, on the Irish emigrants, and on the rebellious characters who managed to get down a good deal of strong liquor even in those godly days. Occasionally there is a touching glimpse of the bareness of the American scene in those years—"villages with a single long street lined with trees, so straight and wide that you can see a chicken run across it a mile off." One of the most moving refrains in the Journal is his hunger for music—"I would be drunk, drunk, drunk, dead drunk to this world with it forever." And though it is the fashion these days to exaggerate Concord's hospitality to the arts, it is made clear by the Journal that if Thoreau made so much of the music in the telegraph wires, "the telegraph harp," as he so lovingly calls it over and again, it was because there was not much other music to listen to. "I have lain awake at night many a time to think of the barking of a dog which I had heard long before, bathing my being again in those waves of sound, as a frequenter of the opera might lie awake remembering the music he had heard."

But by and large the Journal is the attempt to shape into words the vision he took back from his walks, a testing-ground for his art, and a commentary on the journal itself—that is, on the necessities of his character. What he sought from those walks he very consciously defined to himself in 1857, after twenty years of the Journal, in one of those sentences which are so heartbreaking in their truthfulness, for when you read it you realize not only that he has said everything he means, but that he has put his whole life into that sentence. "I come to my solitary woodland walk as the homesick go home."

In this same passage, however, he added with his usual canny awareness of the type he represents in history, "I suppose that this value, in my case, is equivalent to what others get by churchgoing and prayers." As a statement of the facts this is altogether more deft than accurate. Though Thoreau was genuinely and even profoundly mystical, God did not occupy his mind to that extent; it was writing he cared about first, not a belief. But what such nimble and all too often repetitive analyses of his character point up so sharply is that he spent much more time painting himself as Concord's leading crank than on following to the depths the stunning originality of his nature.

Contrary to the usual belief from Emerson and Lowell on, that Thoreau was too intractable, "not enough in touch with his fellow man," I would say that the great fault in his writing, and indeed the real pathos of his life, is that he was all too aware of what other men would think of him. Had he not been so, he could never have written "Walden," which is exhilarating precisely because of its defiance and far more self-dramatizing than even "Leaves of Grass." But Thoreau had an even more deeply original quality to him than "Walden" reveals; you see it in the Journal over and over again—a quality that was perhaps best described by the French mystical writer Simone Weil when she said that "attentiveness without an object is prayer in its supreme form." Only the very purest and most solitary writers have had the gift of such attentiveness; to be alive entirely to the creation itself. But for many reasons, not least of which was the fact that Thoreau was so much the end of a tradition that he had to retrace it for himself, he went to nature as his formal vocation, a background to his quest, something that would support his picture of himself. "Nature" itself was not his chief interest; he was so entirely subjective that he distrusted scientific method even when used by others. But he was looking for a subject; that is, for an opportunity. And of course he could always find a subject in himself. But by constantly dwelling on how different he was, he tended to become uncharacteristically smug about who he was.

Still, without these excited daily inroads into the fields, Thoreau could never have found the measure for his prose. It is a prose, like Hemingway's and Faulkner's, that most characteristically defines the American in literature. We have had greater or at least more comprehensive writers, but none who with such deep intuition grasped in their solitariness the secret of the wilderness, of the legendary unoccupied Western lands, the very tone of man's battle in America against empty space. Emerson had given the call. It was Thoreau who went out and tried it: who wrote as if a sentence were not even true unless you heard it first ring against the ground.

[1951]

It is only in recent years that much attention has been paid to Thoreau as a scientist. The first thorough study was that by Edward S. Deevey, Jr., in his "A Re-Examination of Thoreau's Walden" in the Quarterly Journal of Biology, *XVII (March, 1942), 1-11, in which he presented Thoreau as a pioneer limnologist. The present article by two graduate students at the University of Wisconsin, Mr. Whitford in ecology and Mrs. Whitford in American literature, presents a broader picture of Thoreau's scientific methods and accomplishments.*

THOREAU: PIONEER ECOLOGIST AND CONSERVATIONIST

BY PHILIP AND KATHRYN WHITFORD

Despite the scathing remarks of Lowell in regard to Thoreau's nature studies, of Fannie Hardy Eckstorm in regard to his woodcraft, and of Bradford Torrey in regard to his ornithology, modern scientists have gradually come to claim Thoreau as one of themselves. It is our purpose to examine Thoreau's right to the title of plant ecologist and conservationist, and it is therefore necessary first to determine, if possible, Thoreau's relationship to the plant science of his own day.

Modern taxonomy dates from the time of Linnaeus' use of the "natural system" of classification. This system was modified by the concept of development, or evolution, into the modern phylogenetic classification, a modification which was taking place during Thoreau's lifetime under the leadership of such men as De Can-

From *Scientific Monthly*, LXXIII (November, 1951), 291-96, by permission.

dolle, Torrey, Darwin, and Gray. It is important to note that Thoreau allied himself with these men by his acceptance of the theory of development.

Plant geography was the nearest approach in Thoreau's time to the science of ecology. The exploratory and taxonomic work of such men as Bartram, in America, and Humboldt in South America, was being consolidated in studies that attempted to define the boundaries of the distributions of the world's flora and to determine the conditions and limitations of plant migration. Within Thoreau's lifetime the controversy over migration or specific creation remained unsettled unless one accepts Darwin's *Origin of Species* as the agent of immediate settlement. Thoreau died in 1862 without having read *The Origin of Species*. In this controversy Thoreau rejected the hypothesis of special creation.

Conservation, in Thoreau's day, was not a science, but merely the dream of a few farsighted men and the passion of a group of sentimentalists allied to men like Alcott who were vegetarians because they could not bear to be charged with the destruction of animal life. Ecology as a science was completely unheard of in Thoreau's lifetime, although some taxonomists and plant geographers were contributing work on habitats and associations that served to place them among the precursors of ecology. To this group Thoreau unofficially belonged.

Although the ferment of evolution and specific creation had a place in almost all thinking, scientific or ecclesiastical, in Thoreau's day, Thoreau seems to have taken little part in it. He mentions Darwin several times, but always in connection with the *Voyage of a Naturalist Around the World*. There are no references to Lamarck's earlier studies on acquired characteristics. It seems probable that he was somewhat acquainted with the *Vestiges of Creation* even if only at second hand, for Alcott criticized it to a group at Cambridge in 1854, and in a diary entry a few days earlier records that he and Thoreau sat up talking about "genesis" —a term Alcott used in this pre-Darwin period to designate the concept of change. Thoreau's reading of geology, however, would have introduced him to the controversy, though probably his strongest link with the conflict in this country was Louis Agassiz, for whom he took fish and turtles in the Concord River and Walden Pond. The correspondence with James Elliot Cabot, who was cooperating with Agassiz in his work on American fishes, indicates that Thoreau sent specimens during 1847, many of them at Agassiz's request, and that some of them, at least, had previously been unidentified. In addition to the correspondence about fish, which was conducted largely with Cabot, Thoreau met Agassiz at Concord, where Agassiz came "more than once" and examined turtles with him.

The possible influence of Agassiz cannot be overlooked in any attempt to account for Thoreau's acceptance of the developmental point of view in natural history, for though Agassiz was an advocate of special creation to account for the geographic distribution of species, his work in morphology was based on the concept of development. It would be strange if the subject had not arisen when the two men examined turtles together, for Cabot had written: "The snapping turtles are very interesting to him [Agassiz] as forming a transition from the turtle proper to the alligator and crocodile."

Certainly by October 1860, when Thoreau was puzzling over how new lilies had become established in a small pool in Beck Stow's swamp, he had accepted the theory of development almost without reservation:

I think that we are warranted only in supposing that the former [the new pool] was stocked in the same way as the latter and that there was not a sudden new creation, — at least since the first: yet I have no doubt that peculiarities more or less considerable have thus been gradually produced in the lilies planted in various pools, in consequence of these various conditions, though they all came originally from one seed.

We find ourselves in a world that is already planted, but which is also still being planted as at first. We say of some plants that they grow in wet places and of others that they grow in desert places. The truth is that their seeds are scattered almost everywhere, but here only do they succeed.

Unless you can show me the pool where the lily was created, I shall believe that the oldest fossil lilies which the geologist has detected

. . . originated in that locality in a similar manner to these of Beck Stow's. . . .

The development theory implies a greater vital force in nature, because it is more flexible and accommodating, and equivalent to a sort of constant new creation. *(Journal, 14, 145 [1906])*.

The evidence of the above paragraph cited from Thoreau also goes far to prove that, at a time when even Asa Gray was employing a teleological approach, Thoreau was capable of analyzing plant migration in terms that contain no teleological implication, so that the later Thoreau sometimes approached the most modern ecological thought in this respect. That this was not always the case is vividly illustrated by W. L. McAtee's article entitled "Adaptationist Naivete (*Sci. Monthly,* 48, 253 [1939]), in which he uses Thoreau as an example of the teleological thought implicit in much of the doctrine of protective adaptation. But Thoreau kept excellent scientific company even in his lapses, for McAtee goes on to say, "It is of interest that the suggestions here quoted and numerous others in his *Journal* considerably antedate those of Belt, Wallace, and Darwin—authors usually regarded as the founders of the adaptationist school."

Passing from the ideological basis of Thoreau's ecology to a consideration of his more specific interests, it is apparent that after the period in which Thoreau was primarily interested in the transcendental implications of nature, there is a long period which may be denoted as a time of orientation, or survey. During this time he devoted himself to identifying plants and noting their habitat groups. Bradford Torrey observes that the *Journals* are the record of Thoreau's study, not the product of an accomplished naturalist, and that even though he was more successful in recognizing and naming plants than birds, there is an abundance of question marks sprinkled after the plant denominations. This is quite true, but it is to be noted to Thoreau's credit as a scientist that he placed such question marks after species of which he could not be certain; and it is also to be noted that the largest number of such question marks appear after the names of grasses, sedges, and rushes, after which many a modern ecologist who is not work-

ing specifically with those families is content to write "sp.,"
meaning that the species was not identified. The fact of the matter
is that many members of these families can be identified even
today only after careful examination under a microscope, and
then only when fruits are present. Thoreau's question marks in
many cases are thus a mark of his integrity rather than an indica-
tion that he was not adept at identification.

The most readily observed scientific efforts of Thoreau during
this preliminary period are his phenological records. Although
such observations are common among people who live close to
the land, Thoreau was the first man in this country to keep
extended records of his observations, a fact that led Aldo Leopold
to refer to him as the "father of American phenology." From the
phenological lists which occupy much of the space in the early
Journals and are that part of Thoreau's nature study most frequently reproduced in books for nature enthusiasts, Thoreau
entered the realm of the ecologist proper by adding to his phenological data his lists of habitat groups. The combining of the two
interests is illustrated vividly in such paragraphs as the following:

> The epigaea is not quite out. The earliest peculiarly woodland herba-
> ceous flowers are epigaea, anemone, thalictrum, and — by the first
> of May, Viola pedata. These grow quite in the woods amid dry leaves,
> nor do they depend so much on water as the earliest flowers.

This paragraph serves also to remind one of Francis Allen's
caution not to assume that Thoreau wrote everything he knew in
his *Journal*. He obviously did not. There are frequent sentences
in the *Journals* that have no reference to preceding entries but
which refer to questions in Thoreau's mind. Even when all the
information is present in the *Journal* it is often present in fragments; yet there is evidence that there was a synthesis in Thoreau's
mind. Thus in the excerpt just quoted there is a synthesis of
Thoreau's early observation of the growth of certain *Carex* species,
skunk cabbage, and marsh marigold in and around springs, with
his observation of woodland species.

Like a modern ecologist Thoreau was as much interested in
the plants characteristic of certain locations as in rare or atypical

plants; and it was these characteristic plants that were usually distinguished and noted on his walks. The *Journals* are full of such entries as this one:

> On the first, or westerly, part of the Great Meadows, i.e., the firmer parts and the bank, I find, mixed with sedges of different kinds, much red top (coloring the surface extensively), fowl-meadow (just begun to bloom and of a purplish lead-color, taller than the red top), the slender purple-spiked panic, Agrostis (perennans? or scabra??) In the wet, or main part, besides various other sedges, — as Carex stellulata, lanuginosa, stricta, etc. etc., — wool-grass, now in flower, a sedge (apparently Campullacea var. urticulata toward Holbrook's) thicker culmed than wool-grass, but softer and not round, with fertile spikes often three inches long, and slender. A great part of the meadow is covered with, I think, either this or wool-grass (not in flower). I am not certain which prevails, but I think wool-grass. . . .

The most extensive of such entries are the pages in the appendix of *The Maine Woods,* in which he listed the typical flora of the woods, river and lake shores, the water, and swamps, together with lists of the typical understory of the woods and the shrubs and small trees of the swamps and shores. These lists are uniformly composed of the dominant species of those sites. The next section of the appendix, however, is devoted simply to lists of the species which "I noticed in the Maine woods, in the years 1853 and 1857."

Shorter, but otherwise similar, habitat groups are recorded on his trip along Cape Cod, but the sand made Cape vegetation sparse, and the lists are short enough to be included in the body of the work. The lists from Mount Monadnock are interesting in comparison with those from the Maine woods, because here Thoreau is concerned with the flora of the mountaintop. In many ways this flora was even less familiar to him than that of Maine and seemingly for that reason his comparisons are sometimes more fully expressed, and he makes the attempt to list the plants in "the order of commonness." The chief difference in his approach to such abundance lists and that of a modern ecologist is that Thoreau's is subjective; one tree composition count in Conantum Swamp and one quadrat count of *Houstonia* are his closest approaches to the objective method. Thoreau's most fully stated comparison of sites occurs here also, together with his partial explanation of why similar species should grow in such widely differing sites as a swamp and a mountaintop.

> Though there is little or no soil upon the rocks, owing apparently to the coolness, if not moisture, you have rather the vegetation of a swamp than that of sterile rocky ground below. For example, of the six prevailing trees and shrubs — low blueberry, black spruce, lambkill, black choke-berry, wild holly, and Viburnum nudum — all but the first are characteristic of swampy and low ground, to say nothing of the commonness of wet mosses, the two species of cottongrass, and some other plants of the swamps and meadow.

Such paragraphs go far to prove that Thoreau's interest lay not in the lists alone, but in explanations that would reconcile the lists.

Despite the conspicuous place which phenological and habitat lists hold in the *Journals* of the middle and early years, they were partially displaced in the last three volumes of the *Journal* by Thoreau's preoccupation with the springs and rivers of the Concord region, and his growing concern for the Concord woodlots. Temperature records of the springs and rivers, observations of water plants, of current and cuttings of the rivers, of high water and low, occupy many pages of Volumes XII and XIII, in spite of the fact that in editing Thoreau's writings Bradford Torrey omitted most of Thoreau's study of the physiography of the Concord River. It is unfortunate, of course, for the purposes of this discussion that the complete data are not available, for from that given it is not always possible to trace Thoreau's purpose; yet it was from the partial evidence available that E. S. Deevey, Jr., concluded that Thoreau had made an independent discovery of the stratification of water, and made the correct deduction that such a stratification would affect the distribution of fish.

Inspired by his farmer neighbors, who kept asking him to explain why when they cut off a stand of hardwood in a woodlot it was replaced by pitch pine, and when they cut a pine stand the same ground came up to hardwoods as a rule, Thoreau began his intensive study of the woodlots of the Concord region. Much of the background material for such a study had already been gathered in his years of daily walks in all the Concord region, and in his analysis of tree growth he could draw upon this reserve of knowledge of the region's history and habitat differences. He knew, for instance, that the huge chestnuts he observed in some of the woods and along pastures were probably relics of the more ancient woods of Concord, and he made lists of the sites that seemed most favorable to the common tree species. Then he turned his attention to seeding, since he did not believe, as many of his contemporaries did, in spontaneous generation or in special creations to account for the distribution of species in the world.

I suppose that most have seen — at any rate I can show them — English cherry trees, so called, coming up not uncommonly in our woods and under favorable circumstances becoming full-grown trees. Now I think they will not pretend that they came up there in the same manner before this country was discovered by the whites. But if cherry trees come up by spontaneous generation, why should they not have sprung up there in that way a thousand years ago as well as now?

If the pine seed is spontaneously generated why is it not produced in the Old World as well as in America? I have no doubt that it can be raised from seed in corresponding situations there, and that it will seem to spring up just as mysteriously there as it does here. Yet if it will grow so *after* the seed has been carried thither, why should it not before, if the seed is unnecessary to its production?

The above-mentioned cherry trees come up, though they are comparatively few, just like the red cherry, and no doubt the same persons would consider them spontaneously generated. But why did nature defer raising that species here by spontaneous generation until we had raised it from stones? (*Journal*, 14, 333 [1906]).

Thoreau also rejected the theory that seeds lie in the ground for many years awaiting an opportunity favorable for their germination and growth. This left two obvious methods of reproduction —stump sprouts around recently cut trees and seed of comparatively recent origin. He began to observe sproutings from stumps and came to the conclusion that he could sometimes detect a wood which had been cut three times by the positions of trees which were obviously old stump sprouts.

Thus I can easily find in countless numbers in our forests, frequently in the third succession, the stumps of oaks which were cut near the end of the last century. Perhaps I can recover thus generally the oak woods of the beginning of the last century, if the land has remained in woodland. I have an advantage over the geologists for I can not only detect the order of events but the time during which they elapsed, by counting the rings on the stumps. Thus you can unroll the rotten papyrus on which the history of the Concord forest is written (14, 152).

Of course, the gradual manner in which many woodlots are cut — often only thinned out — must affect the truth of my statements in numerous instances. The regularity of the succession will be interfered with and what is true of one end of a lot will not be true of the other (14, 152).

This concern with stumps and stump sprouts, in conjunction with his knowledge of the chestnuts, seems for a time to have led him to contemplate the further problem of whether he could not "recover" the woods of Concord—that is, work out the history of the woods he was observing and possibly map them by his knowledge of growth methods and the successional pattern of the region. This was one of the plans of which there are frequent hints in the last volume of the *Journal,* but his early death left him no opportunity to expand the design. His observation of stump sprouts, however, led him to the conclusion that, though a woodlot reforested by stump sprouts was a faster and easier source of wood for the farmer than one produced from seed, in the long run the forest produced on sproutland was inferior to the one that came from seed; for the new trees were more subject to the diseases of old trees. He wondered, indeed, whether the vitality of the stock were not eventually vitiated; for in inspecting a woods which he believed had been cut for the third time and each previous time allowed to come up to sproutland he could find almost no new stump sprouts. This lack of sprouts on old sproutland did not explain the succession he was concerned with, but he noted in his *Journal* that for his own part he would prefer a woodlot which had its origin in seed rather than sprouts. He concluded that woodlot management could be improved in Concord by a study of the history of the woods concerned.

Thoreau was, of course, familiar with the practice of crop

rotation in agriculture, and he never entirely dismissed from his theories a belief that succession represented a crop rotation in nature—that once the seed of white or pitch pine, for instance, became established on land from which the hardwoods had been cut these new trees throve better than wood hardwoods because the "soil was new to them." But the mechanism of succession still evaded him, and he turned his attention to the seeds themselves. He gathered acorns from the white, scarlet, and black oaks of the region and placed them in a drawer for six months or so and then examined them again. Almost none were firm and viable. He observed the results of an acorn blight and the periodicity of pine seeding. Obviously one factor which would determine the growth of seedlings on newly cleared land was what type of seed had been abundant and viable in the season of cutting, but he was aware of other factors as well, as his observation of maple seedlings attests.

I see where a great many little red maples have sprung up in a potato field, apparently since the last plowing or cultivating this year. They extend thickly as much as 11 rods in a north west direction from a small tree, the only red maple in that neighborhood. It is evidently owing to the land having been cultivated this year that the seed vegetated there; otherwise there would now be no evidence that any such seeds had fallen here. Last year and for many years it has been a pasture. It is evident that land may be kept in pasture and covered with grass any number of years, and though there are maples adjacent to it, none of the seed will catch in it; but at last it is plowed, and this year the seed which falls on it germinates and if it chances not to be plowed again, and the cattle are kept out, you soon have a maple wood there. So of other light seeded trees (14, 71).

The distribution of pine seeds like that of maples presented no problem. Such seeds were light enough to be carried by the wind, and he concluded that they were everywhere available in the Concord area. The seeds of hardwoods were a different matter. Either he had to account for their distribution or accept the theory that acorns actually did lie dormant in the ground, as many of his neighbors claimed, for fifty or a hundred years—or perhaps longer than that. Squirrels, of course, carried nuts and so did other animals, but did they carry away enough in a single season and then leave them uneaten to account for the seeding of an entire wood? It seemed unlikely—even though Thoreau reasoned that such animals would tend to carry the nuts to a pine woods, which provided greater protection from the winter wind than did the woods in which they grew. This at best was but a partial solution. He extended his observations to include seedlings as well as seed and here made a discovery that satisfied him. He pulled up a small oak seedling one day in walking through a pine lot. Its root was heavy and thick with the growth of several years. The next day he went to all the neighboring pine lots and pulled oak seedlings in each one. Almost invariably they had the fusiform roots of several years' growth—sometimes of as much as seven years. The pine seedlings had no such roots. He then went to oak woods and looked for pine seedlings but he found only very young ones; and then the picture began to clarify. If a pine wood were cut the little oaks which had survived for several years in their shelter were released to the light and had several years' head start over pine seedlings of the year of cutting. Thus the likelihood was that the resultant cutting would come up to hardwoods. In the case of hardwoods being cut the more abundant seed of the pines was likely to produce a pine stand. That explanation, in brief, was what he presented to the Middlesex Agricultural Association as his solution, but his *Journal* supplies the obvious conditioning influences and makes readers aware that Thoreau had not ignored these further factors. If a farmer cut a pine woods and then burned the land, he destroyed the little oaks. Thus in all likelihood he would get a pine stand. Thoreau thought he would do better to let the oaks come up. The "land was pine sick."

Interested as he was in cutover land and the occurrence of stump sprouts, Thoreau's next step was almost inevitable. He became interested in stump rings; and since it should never be forgotten that Thoreau was a practical Yankee before he became a transcendentalist it follows that his interest in stump rings, like his interest in succession, was stimulated by his concern for proper woodlot management. At what age, he asked now, is it most profitable to cut trees? He turned to his measurements of pine stumps and analyzed them. He concluded that they grew

... from first to last about a fifteenth of an inch a year. But they grew very slowly indeed for the last fifty or more years. They did nearly half (?) of their growing in the first third of their existence ... I should say that they averaged one thirty-sixth part of an inch the third or last fifty years. That is, their rate of growth the three successive periods of fifty years diminishes in geometrical progression, the quotient being two ...
... but I have not yet taken into account the fact that, though the thickness of the layer is less, its superficies, or extent is greater, as the diameter of the tree increases. Let us compare the three portions of the wood. If the diameter at the end of the first fifty years is four, the second fifty, six, and the third, seven, then the amount of wood added each term will be (to omit very minute fractions) twelve and a half, fifteen and a half, and ten, respectively. So that, though in the second fifty the rings are twice as near together, yet considerably more wood is produced than in the first, but in the third fifty the tree is evidently enfeebled, and it probably is not profitable (so far as bulk is concerned) to let it grow any more (14, 205).

The stump-ring counts and analysis were in progress at the time of Thoreau's death. In fact, he caught the lingering cold which hastened the family malady, tuberculosis, by kneeling in a wet snow to count stump rings. These notes were not among those which Thoreau spent the final months of his life arranging for publication—probably because he knew no source which would publish them, whereas for such essays as "Walking" and "Winter Apples" there was already a market. Therefore this material remained buried in the *Journals* until 1906 when the *Journals* were published nearly in full. For the same reason Thoreau's often bitter indictment of the manner in which woods and woodlots were managed remained unpublished. As has already been pointed out, there was no public interest in conservation during Thoreau's lifetime. He belonged to the period of the great despoilers of land, not its conservators; yet his own preoccupation with the little world of Concord bestowed a value upon that land which was commensurate with present estimates of land value.

Thoreau wondered, though casually, whether more nutriment was not washed off the brow of a cultivated hill than could be replaced by manuring, but his chief concern was reserved for the woodlots.

> The time will soon come, if it has not already, when we shall have to take special pains to secure and encourage the growth of white oaks, as we already must that of chestnuts for the most part. These oaks will become so scattered that there will not be seed enough to seed the ground rapidly and completely (14, 133).

> What shall we say to the management that halts between two courses, — does neither this nor that but botches both? I see many a pasture on which the pitch or white pines are spreading where the bush-whack is from time to time used with a show of vigor, and I despair of my trees, — I say mine, for the farmer evidently does not mean they shall be his, — and yet this questionable work is so poorly done that those very fields grow steadily greener and more forestlike from year to year in spite of cows and bush-whack, till at length the farmer gives up the contest from sheer weariness, and finds himself the owner of a wood-lot. Now whether wood-lots or pastures are most profitable for him I will not undertake to say, but I am certain that a wood-lot and a pasture combined is not profitable (14, 145).

> The history of a wood-lot is often, if not commonly, here, a history of cross purposes, — of steady and consistent endeavor on the part of Nature, of interference and blundering with a glimmering of intelligence at the eleventh hour on the part of the proprietor. The proprietor of a wood-lot commonly treats Nature as an Irishman does a horse, — by standing in front of him and beating him in the face all the way across a field (14, 132).

> We are so accustomed to see another forest spring up immediately as a matter of course, whether from the stump or from seed, when a forest is cut down, never troubling about the succession, that we hardly associate the seed with the tree, and do not anticipate the time when this regular succession will cease and we shall be obliged to plant, as they do in all old countries. The planters of Europe must have a very different, a much correcter, notion of the value of the seed of forest trees than we (14, 70).

Thus the charge that Thoreau "tried to see with the inside of his eye too often" loses weight when it is set against the evidence of his researches, and Thoreau is seen as a naturalist who, in a day that was predominantly interested in the discovery and naming of species, was making an effort to synthesize and apply his knowledge of one small area of the country. The lack of statistical analysis, which is the quality a modern ecologist would criticize first, was a lack shared by all biological sciences in Thoreau's day. It is probably this lack that has caused Thoreau to be accepted slowly as a scientist, for, though his work was done before 1862, much of it was not known until the *Journals* were published in 1906, and by that time the concept of science had undergone the radical changes which brought increasing emphasis upon statistical analysis of vegetation. It is interesting to note, however, that the men of literature who as a group have made the most exhaustive studies of Thoreau have been the last to accept him as a man of science. He has been claimed as one of the first conservationists; he has been claimed as a limnologist, and as the "father of American phenology;" his essay on the "Succession of Forest Trees" has been accorded a place in the *Bibliography of North American Forestry,* but only Raymond Adams and Joseph Wood Krutch in the field of American literature have applied to him the term "ecologist," and then only in the most general terms.